Change management in TVET colleges
Lessons learnt from the field of practice

Edited by
André Kraak, Andrew Paterson and Kedibone Boka

Published in 2016 by African Minds
4 Eccleston Place, Somerset West, 7130, Cape Town, South Africa
info@africanminds.org.za
www.africanminds.org.za

and

JET Education Services,
The Education Hub, 6 Blackwood Avenue, Parktown, Johannesburg, South Africa
www.jet.org.za

© 2016 African Minds

All contents of this document, unless specified otherwise, are licensed under a Creative Commons Attribution 4.0 International License.

The views expressed in this publication are those of the authors. When quoting from any of the chapters, readers are requested to acknowledge the relevant author.

Print edition: 978-1-928331-33-9
eBook edition: 978-1-928331-34-6
ePub edition: 978-1-928331-35-3

Copies of this book are available for free download at:
www.africanminds.org.za
www.jet.org.za

ORDERS
African Minds
Email: info@africanminds.org.za

Or JET Education Services
Email: info@jet.org.za

To order printed books from outside Africa, please contact:
African Books Collective
PO Box 721, Oxford OX1 9EN, UK
Email: orders@africanbookscollective.com

Copy-editor: Maureen Mosselson
Cover photograph: Hannelie Coetzee, with thanks to the Eastcape Midlands College, Brickfields Road Campus, and the students.

Designed and produced by COMPRESS.dsl | www.compressdsl.com

Contents

Acronyms and abbreviations iv

Introduction: Perspectives on programmes, projects and policies in the TVET colleges
Andrew Paterson vii

CHAPTER 1
Three decades of restructuring in further education colleges: Divergent outcomes across differing global vocational education and training systems
André Kraak 1

CHAPTER 2
Unfinished business: Managing the transformation of further education and training colleges
Anthony Gewer 23

CHAPTER 3
Throwing good money after bad: Barriers South African vocational teachers experience in becoming competent educators
Ronel Blom 47

CHAPTER 4
A climate for change? Vertical and horizontal collegial relations in TVET colleges
Volker Wedekind and Zanele Buthelezi 64

CHAPTER 5
Preparing TVET college graduates for the workplace: Employers' views
Joy Papier, Seamus Needham, Nigel Prinsloo and Timothy McBride 83

CHAPTER 6
What will it take to turn TVET colleges around? Evaluation of a large-scale college improvement programme
Carmel Marock, Eleanor Hazell and Bina Akoobhai 103

Acronyms and abbreviations

BANKSETA	Banking Sector Education and Training Authority
BEd	Bachelor of Education degree
BTEC	Business and Technology Education Council
BVE Raad	Netherlands Association of VET Colleges
CAP	Competency and Placement
CCF	Colleges Collaboration Fund
Cedefop	European Centre for the Development of Vocational Training
CFO	chief financial officer
CIP	Colleges Improvement Programme
COVE	Centre of Vocational Excellence
DANIDA	Danish International Development Agency
DBE	Department of Basic Education
DEDT	Department of Economic Development and Tourism
DET	Department of Education and Training
DHET	Department of Higher Education and Training
DoE	Department of Education
DoL	Department of Labour
ELRC	Education Labour Relations Council
EMIS	education management information systems
ET	education and training
FE	further education
FET	further education and training
FETI	Further Education and Training Institute
FIETA	Forest Industries Education and Training Authority
FoodBev SETA	Food and Beverages Manufacturing SETA
GCSE	General Certificate of Secondary Education
GSCE (AS)	General Senior Certificate of Education advanced subsidiary
HAVO	senior general secondary education
HBO	professional higher education
HR	human resources
HRD	human resource development
ICT	information and communications technology
ILO	International Labour Organization
IPSS	Institute for Post-School Studies
IT	information technology
JET	JET Education Services
LSC	Learning and Skills Council
LWIB	Local Workforce Investment Board

M&E	monitoring and evaluation
MBO	secondary vocational education
MEC	Member of Executive Committee
merSETA	Manufacturing, Engineering and Related Services SETA
NATED	National Accredited Technical Education Diploma
NBI	National Business Initiative
NCV	National Certificate Vocational
NPM	new public management
NQF	National Qualifications Framework
NSF	National Skills Fund
NSFAS	National Student Financial Aid Scheme
NTSI	National Training Strategy Initiative
NVQ	National vocational qualification
OBE	outcomes-based education
OECD	Organisation for Economic Cooperation and Development
OPR	out-to-purpose review
PEDs	provincial education departments
PIVOTAL	Professional, Vocational, Technical and Academic Learning
QCTO	Quality Council for Trade and Occupations
ROCs	Regional Occupational Colleges
RSA	Republic of South Africa
SACE	South African Council for Educators
SAICA	South African Institute of Chartered Accountants
SANQF	South African National Qualifications Framework
SETA	Sector Education and Training Authority
SFA	Skills Funding Agency
SSACI	Swiss-South African Cooperation Initiative
SSC	Sector Skills Council
SSS	student support services
TVET	technical and vocational education and training
UKCES	United Kingdom Commission on Employment
UNESCO	United Nations Educational, Scientific and Cultural Organisation
VET	vocational education and training
VMBO	preparatory vocational education
VWO	pre-university education
WBE	workplace-based experience
WEB	Wet Educatie en Beroepsonderwijs
WIL	work-integrated learning
WO	university education

Introduction

PERSPECTIVES ON PROGRAMMES, PROJECTS AND POLICIES IN THE TVET COLLEGES

Andrew Paterson
Executive Manager, Research and Planning,
JET Education Services

Introduction

The South African Technical and Vocational Education and Training (TVET) colleges (formerly the Further Education and Training or 'FET colleges') seem to embody a fundamental institutional enigma – despite multiple changes intended to improve the quality and efficiency of the colleges, they are still viewed as underperforming, perhaps even impervious to change efforts.

In this context, JET Education Services (JET) was commissioned to conduct the Colleges Improvement Programme (CIP)[1] between 2011 and 2014 in fifteen selected colleges in the Eastern Cape and Limpopo provinces. The idea for this book was conceived during the time when JET teams were in the field.

This collection of papers represents an effort to make sense of the enigma of the colleges from various perspectives, with the aim of contributing to a better understanding of why the cumulative effect of changes in the colleges have combined to generate unexpected, if not disappointing, results. An argument commonly advanced is that the colleges have been inundated by changes that over time have contributed to a condition of malaise and discontent. Too many changes compressed into a short time-space will ultimately become counterproductive as the absorptive capacity of institutions comes under stress, but claiming this condition as the sole cause carries insufficient explanatory value. Limitations on the impact of interventions may be introduced through the policy and planning directives and implementation plans. Policy-driven institutional changes from central or regional government may have design flaws, or may bring about unintended consequences that constrain or contradict the desired changes. Then it may be that well conceptualised change breaks down because implementation is faulty, leading to insipid buy-in and low adoption.

Each time a new intervention is contemplated, quite complex institutional conditions that vary from college to college must be taken into account. The bricolage of local circumstance will shape how colleges respond to each new intervention. This realisation generates an implicit challenge, which is to be able to design an intervention that will have institutional specificity while aspiring to system-wide benchmarks for improvement and performance.

The challenge of designing and implementing a programme in institutions that have been in a seemingly constant state of change or transition motivated this book which attempts to identify, separate, and analyse key influences on change in the TVET colleges.

The complexity of the colleges' responses to change initiatives contributes to the enigma that is the TVET colleges. This characteristic creates grounds for questions regarding programme design and implementation, for instance: What is the most appropriate intervention design and intensity? How much must the design be adapted, institution by institution? Is overarching support and administration sufficient? What preconditions must be achieved before certain interventions can be implemented in some colleges?

---

1   Though it was named the Colleges Improvement Project, its scale and long-term intervention timescale made it preferable to refer to the CIP as a programme.

What interventions must start from within the college – from the inside out – and what interventions must be initiated from the outside in? Lastly, in what sequence should interventions in the colleges be introduced? These fundamental questions are raised because this edited book is presented as a means of opening up important debate on how TVET college institutional change should be undertaken. This is not a new discussion, but one that has accompanied the series of changes brought about in colleges over the past three decades.

Accordingly, chapters in this collection address: the political economy of TVET types in different countries which, by comparison, illuminate the South African case; a periodisation of government interventions in the TVET sector over the last three decades; the unsettled state and status of TVET lecturers in relation to their job requirements and conditions of service; and the halting evolution of collegial relationships between college lecturers towards higher collegiality; and employer expectations of college graduates and how colleges are responding.

These chapters were selected because they:

- Highlight key perspectives from macro- to micro- through international comparative study and interrogate how macro-economic and political factors shape TVET systems;
- Provide a perspective on the quality, timing, impacts, and outcomes of government policy, identify key government policy and implementation features, and evaluate their overall impact;
- Bring to light the experience of TVET lecturers who are central participants in any proposal to renovate colleges by unpacking the formal and informal structures which facilitate and constrain TVET lecturer development and revealing fragmentation of lecturer collegial relations which detract from individual and institutional development;
- Draw on employers' perspectives about the preparedness of TVET college graduates seeking work in their respective sectors; and
- Bring forward insights about the monitoring and evaluation of the CIP.

This introductory chapter proceeds as follows:

- First, it presents a metaphor for change in the colleges based on the physics of ocean waves. Waves are taken to represent programmes, policies, or projects aimed at bringing about change in the colleges.
- Second, it briefly introduces the most important underlying assumption of change in the TVET colleges, which is to massively increase enrolment in the immediate short term, to be sustained over the next decade and more. This assumption is placed in juxtaposition with the seemingly unending challenge of imbuing colleges with commitment to financial probity and which undercuts confidence in progressive institutional development.
- Third, it presents an account of the Colleges Improvement Project (CIP) as background to the six substantive chapters. The particular focus of the CIP intervention was on teaching and learning. As such, the CIP contributes a teaching and learning-

focused perspective to the collection of chapters and, while teaching and learning are not explicitly covered, the themes addressed in these chapters do have an impact on teaching and learning.
- Fourth, this introduction briefly summarises each of the contributed chapters and draws links between them, touching on the overarching debates.

Waves of change

TVET colleges have been exposed to various forms of change over the past twenty years. The changes have involved rationalisation of college numbers and size, introduction of new programmes and plans to phase out others, recapitalisation of infrastructure, new forms of college governance, shifts in line-function accountability of colleges, and shifts in staff employment regimes, interspersed with sporadic lecturer training.

In the post-2009 period, colleges have been required to establish or adopt functioning relationships with Sector Education and Training Authorities (SETAs), to pursue collaboration with higher education institutions, and to initiate workable relationships with employers in order to generate opportunities for students and graduates respectively to benefit from experience in workplaces while studying and from work placements upon graduation.

Multiple waves of change have had an impact on the colleges in the period of two decades. The study of ocean waves and fluid dynamics provides a useful physical metaphor for the waves of institutional change to which the colleges have been exposed. Waves work on the ocean floor and coastline to reshape it, while simultaneously the ocean floor and coastline contain and influence the work of the waves. Out of this interaction, the shoreline may be transformed. However, waves do not travel in exactly straight lines and do not arrive at the shore in a straight line, just as a wave of institutional change does not arrive at exactly the same time or work evenly on each institution. In a fluid environment, it is possible for waves to move at different speeds, causing some waves to slow down and allow following waves to catch up. This movement increases the amount of energy that is expended, intensifying the impact of the waves on the sea shore. In the colleges, some waves of change slowed down while others caught up with them, testing the ability of the colleges to cope with the combined impact. Waves respond differently, depending on the shape and characteristics of the sea shore, providing an analogy for how waves of change impact differently, depending on the particular conditions in each college. Finally, when waves begin impacting on the shoreline, they travel at different speeds and in different directions, leading to interference and turbulence which features unpredictable changes. This property of waves is analogous with how interventions may interfere with each other, causing a reduction in effectiveness. An example is the overly high or contradictory demands placed on the colleges' administrative staff.

Expectations for change: Creating the conditions

The burden of change involves expectations of change, then preparation for change, followed by implementation of change. The Department of Higher Education and Training

(DHET) has placed great emphasis on the role of TVET colleges in alleviating and meeting the demand for post-school education, especially among young people who have left school early, attained poor matric results, or who want to obtain vocational skills that might support sustainable livelihoods. In the light of the triple burden of poverty, unemployment, and inequality which disproportionately affects South Africa's youth, there is powerful cause to pressure education and training systems to take on this burden. Though TVET head-count enrolments rose from 345 566 in 2010 and were estimated to be sitting at 650 000 in 2013, the DHET had set targets for head count enrolments of one million by 2015 and 2.5 million by 2030 (DHET, 2013).

These global estimates are formidable indeed, but it is difficult to escape strategies based on expanding TVET, even more so when the share of these institutions in taking on post-school youth lags behind the proportionate commitment from higher education. Data shows that by 2011, the TVET colleges had accomplished a limited enrolment impression of 4.2% on the 19- to 24-year-old age group. This was, by comparison, a small fraction of the participation rates of 18% in 2010 and 19% in 2011 of 20- to 24-year-olds enrolled in the public higher education system (Statistics South Africa, 2013). Even by international standards, South Africa has a disproportionately large group of higher education students enrolled in relation to TVET students. This is in inverse proportion to expected labour market demand in a middle-income country for middle-level skills. The investment pattern that generates this ratio of higher education to college and TVET enrolment is counter-productive to economic growth and skills needs and continues to feed misplaced demand.

Further reason for increasing investment in the TVET sector is evident in the unequal distribution of enrolment opportunity between provinces. Table 1 shows how TVET enrolment in some provinces can be as much as double that of other provinces. Though the location of colleges in relation to provincial boundaries will have distorted the proportions to some extent, this does not detract from an overall picture of inequitable distribution of access.

The high expectations for the TVET colleges to make a superhuman contribution in bringing the sector into alignment with national planning are most certainly daunting. But even more daunting is pressure on the DHET to find a way of coaxing a number of colleges towards implementing appropriate financial controls and accountability. In 2013, nine colleges were under administration. The Finance and Fiscal Commission observed that: 'The sector is facing governance and management problems, especially with regard to financial management. Financial accountability in the sector needs serious attention, to ensure that any additional funding to the sector will be used effectively and efficiently' (Finance and Fiscal Commission, 2013: 36).

Clearly, it is fundamentally important to create the conditions within which TVET institutional change can flourish. The restitution of financial probity remains at the top of the agenda if ambitions for TVET growth are to be achieved. This situation presents a useful point of departure for defining the most appropriate course of action and whether the initiative should come from the inside or from the outside in.

TABLE 1 Participation of 19–24-year-olds in FET college education per province, 2011

Province	19–24-year-olds in the population			19–24-year-olds enrolled in the FET colleges			% of 19–24-year-olds in the population enrolled in the FET colleges		
	Male	Female	Grand Total	Male	Female	Grand Total	Male	Female	Grand Total
Eastern Cape	448 738	448 018	896 756	12 081	12 919	25 000	2.7%	2.9%	2.8%
Free State	167 704	164 129	331 833	10 613	11 379	21 992	6.3%	6.9%	6.6%
Gauteng	567 634	550 238	1 117 872	39 697	28 587	68 284	7.0%	5.2%	6.1%
KwaZulu-Natal	665 025	664 075	1 329 100	22 824	22 334	45 158	3.4%	3.4%	3.4%
Limpopo	362 416	367 273	729 689	15 847	16 608	32 455	4.4%	4.5%	4.4%
Mpumalanga	234 891	230 591	465 482	4 940	5 130	10 070	2.1%	2.2%	2.2%
Northern Cape	63 034	61 508	124 542	2 254	2 400	4 654	3.6%	3.9%	3.7%
North West	187 319	184 296	371 615	6 352	5 532	11 884	3.4%	3.0%	3.2%
Western Cape	276 712	272 694	549 406	14 560	13 964	28 524	5.3%	5.1%	5.2%
All provinces	2 973 473	2 942 822	5 916 295	129 168	118 853	248 021	4.3%	4.0%	4.2%

Source: Finance and Fiscal Commission (2013: 39).

Colleges Improvement Project

Soon after being established in 2009, the DHET began preparations for assuming full oversight and responsibility for the TVET colleges. It was apparent at the time that high levels of dysfunctionality characterised the operations of a number of colleges in which core operational systems were reportedly close to breakdown. The situation was severe enough for the DHET to mobilise urgent action, first to stabilise the situation and then to implement a 'turnaround strategy' aimed at improving functionality and building capacity in the targeted colleges.

These conditions contributed to the DHET's decision to initiate the CIP, aimed at improving the capacity, functionality, and performance of selected colleges in the Eastern Cape and Limpopo. The CIP in Limpopo started some months later than in the Eastern Cape, but interventions in the two provinces were kept in broad alignment.

The CIP became a three-year project in operation between October 2011 and the end of 2014. The DHET appointed JET as the project manager funded through a National Skills Fund (NSF) grant.

The ultimate aim of the CIP was to bring about a turnaround in the performance of fifteen participating colleges in the two provinces. Accordingly, it was important to ensure that the interventions would be institutionalised and could be sustained beyond the life of the project itself.

Project values and principles

The CIP was informed by the value of working collaboratively, which applied to interactions between the main participants, especially the provincial departments of education and then the DHET, which was set to include the TVET colleges within its mandate to administer all of post-school education.[2]

The CIP was underpinned by three principles.

- **Each institution should be understood on its own terms:** This required individual institutional problem diagnosis that would necessitate tailoring interventions from a general menu to specific institutional conditions.
- **The project should be strategy led:** This placed the responsibility on leadership and management of each institution to devise an appropriate institutional strategic plan that would serve as the institution's 'roadmap to transformation'. Each strategic plan should inform the annual performance plans and budgets or operational plans and provide the backdrop for institutional monitoring and evaluation and performance assessment.
- **Accountability for performance should be strengthened:** Accountability would be assessed against implementation of strategic and operational plans, based on a college-wide performance management system, including performance contracts for college principals.

In addition, as the project got under way, JET's teaching and learning interventions evolved according to the principle of commitment to building individual competence and institutional capacity wherever possible by:

- Building systems and capacity to contribute to the long-term improvement of students' performance and employability;
- Improving institutional capacity through better, integrated planning for teaching and learning practice; and
- Improving the competence of the teaching staff.

Further, it was determined that as far as possible, the CIP work programme should be planned so that the programme could be accommodated within the planning and budgeting cycle of the college.

Project focus areas

An initial inception period of six months was agreed to, during which rapid assessments of the status of the colleges were conducted, with specific attention to the CIP focus areas.

---

2 The FET Colleges Amendment Act No. 3 of 2012 provided for provinces to hand over administration of the colleges to the national department, while personnel transfer was completed thereafter in April 2015.

Data and information from the rapid assessment reports were aggregated to establish baselines of the functionality of the colleges in each province.

Originally, there were six functional areas across which the CIP was expected to support the colleges in building policies, processes, systems and capacity (Finance, Governance and Management, Human Resources, Planning and Education Management Information Systems (EMIS), Student Support Services, and Teaching and Learning). Each of these areas is dealt with in the following section:

- The project design made improvements to **teaching and learning** the core focus of programme interventions and concentrated in particular on strategies to strengthen and promote quality teaching and learning and building competencies of students and lecturers.
- Regarding **student support services**, the project aimed to form an integrated system of support to enable students to achieve success in their studies and employability. Targets for achievement as indicated by pass rates and workplace readiness and employability were agreed to.
- The project's approach to **human resources (HR)** included building capacity, competence, and confidence in HR personnel, ensuring that human resources management had the required facilities and technology, that HR had established protocols for working with other units, and that a comprehensive set of policies was in place.
- In the project design, five areas critical to proper **management and governance** at colleges were identified. At the apex of these was building a culture of planning and accountability. Also emphasised was college council leadership in changing the culture of teaching and learning.
- In addressing **EMIS**, the scope of work in the work programme was seen to underpin all other focus areas. Improving EMIS depended on clarifying the roles and responsibilities in EMIS management, asserting the role of EMIS policies and protocols, ensuring functionality and effectiveness of the systems and technology employed for EMIS operation, and compliance management in EMIS.
- The scope of work in the **financial and risk management** area originally included ensuring that a comprehensive set of policies and protocols was in place, with suitable systems and appropriately capacitated staff. This work programme was taken away from the CIP when the DHET entered into a partnership with the South African Institute of Chartered Accountants (SAICA) for the provision of assistance relating to financial management and administration.

The DHET's partnership with SAICA brought additional external assistance to colleges in the areas of finance and human resources. This reduced the spread of focus areas under the responsibility of the CIP to:

- Teaching and learning;
- Student support services;
- Governance and management; and
- EMIS.

The process according to which the CIP focused its operations is represented in the following figure.

FIGURE 1 CIP activities to enhance college functionality

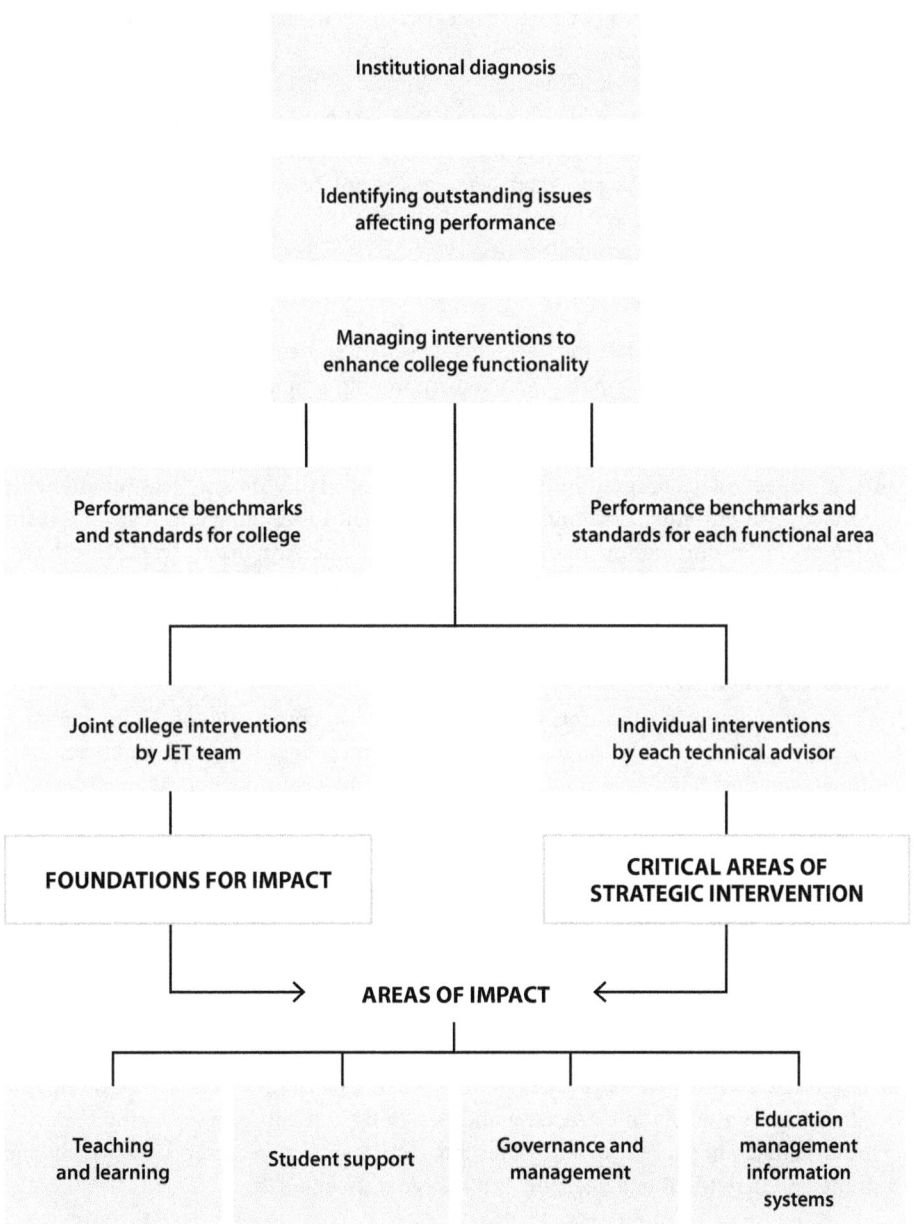

Improved quality of teaching and learning: The centripetal goal of the CIP

The findings of the initial rapid assessment of the colleges revealed that teaching and learning activities were not receiving the level of attention and resources needed to be carried out effectively. Informed by these findings and responding to the overarching objectives of the CIP – to improve the capacity, functionality, and performance of the project colleges – the JET intervention teams sought to reinforce teaching and learning as the core focus and function of TVET colleges central to all aspects of college planning and operations through focused systemic interventions. The bottom line was improving pass rates and improving employability to enable more students to complete their qualifications within a reasonable time frame and to equip them to compete confidently in the labour market. Concurrent CIP programmes brought in specialist technical input to improve the governance and management systems of the colleges as well as data management, monitoring and support, and student support, which were all directed towards supporting teaching and learning.

Student performance

As the project progressed, JET increasingly focused on student performance and success, with the aim of improving pass rates and improving employability – enabling more students to complete their qualifications within a reasonable time frame and equipping them to compete confidently in the labour market. Across the broad scope of the project, different aspects of the programme which were developed to address college functionality – from student enrolment planning and management to teaching and learning in the classroom, from curriculum management to academic support to workplace-based experience – were channelled towards informing and supporting improvements in students' performance.

Lecturer development

Training and support for lecturers formed an important component of the programme. Over the longer term, a solution to the concern around college lecturers' qualifications is required, and the DHET is in the process of developing professional level qualifications and a full qualifications structure for college lecturing staff. Looking at the short to medium term, JET addressed this concern with a number of interventions to strengthen lecturers' capacity and teaching practice, as well as providing support to curriculum managers and staff in the colleges. Since the CIP was limited to three years in duration, the need for a longer-term solution to low levels of college lecturer qualifications was anticipated.

Curriculum systems development

Importantly, the programmes discussed above were extended to support curriculum managers and staff as well, since curriculum services such as advice on incorporating ICT or other learning media into teaching and designing and authoring learning materials can substantially impact the quality of teaching and learning. Lecturer development and training for curriculum management and college staff included:

- Lecturer induction, induction resources for curriculum staff, and induction training workshops;

- Training in assessment and moderation (essential to improving certification rates/pass rates);
- Mathematics topics workshops (for lecturers);
- Imparting best practice in lesson planning and teaching strategies, and facilitating lessons;
- Classroom observation and feedback sessions offering support to lecturers in their teaching practice; and
- Support and mentoring of curriculum managers in implementing plans.

In addition to teaching-related interventions, the CIP also involved systemic developments in related facets of the teaching and learning value chain:

- Facilitating integrated curriculum management;
- Instituting integrated curriculum monitoring and support;
- Training on the use of subject and assessment guidelines; and
- Establishing college and campus performance committees (including academic registrars at central offices and heads of departments at campus level).

Peer tutoring

One of the concerns identified in the rapid assessment of the colleges at the beginning of the CIP was high levels of repeated failure among students in the core subjects of Mathematics and English. This caused students to take more years to graduate and negatively impacted student throughput and certification, raising the per-graduate cost in state subsidy as well as the average private costs of graduation.

The JET project team introduced an innovative approach for improving student's curriculum knowledge and self-confidence. In this case, a student to student peer tutoring intervention that was implemented had positive benefits for students and lecturers.

While Mathematics was the main focus of the CIP peer tutoring programme, English language is also often a serious stumbling block for students, especially in more rural colleges where some lecturers conduct their lectures in the vernacular, even if English is the prescribed teaching medium. This is problematic during examinations, because even if students understood their lectures in whichever subject – Mathematics, Engineering and Physics – in their home language, they might not understand the same material when presented in English in examination papers.

To address these circumstances, particularly in the Mathematics and English language subjects, the CIP first provided Mathematics revision and extra lessons in Saturday classes and during college holidays. However, these raised costs for the colleges in payment for lecturer's services and supervision. In any case, the extra classes were not well attended by students. The successor to this idea was the peer tutoring programme.

The idea of using Level 4 National Certificate Vocational (NVC) students to tutor Level 2 NCV students who were struggling with Mathematics evolved during the course of the project and most of the colleges took up the programme. JET provided support in designing and structuring the tutoring programme. At each campus this involved the senior curriculum manager and the student support services manager. The programme was structured to provide for oversight/supervision, timetabling for tutorials, and the monitoring and recording of attendance and progress. The materials addressed basic Mathematics concepts, which is where the gaps in understanding were found to be. By addressing these gaps and giving students a clear and sound foundational understanding of Mathematics, the tutoring sessions made it easier for students to move on to the higher levels of Mathematics required in TVET courses – particularly in Engineering, Accountancy, and other such studies.

It is important to consider the successes of the peer tutoring programme within the broader CIP. The tutoring programme succeeded in regenerating and promoting a culture of learning. Among students, JET witnessed a renewed enthusiasm for learning, for wanting to do well, and college principals, staff, and lecturers generally responded positively in discussions on the proposed interventions and their implementation. College staff members were responsive to suggestions from the project teams, open to new possibilities, new ways of doing things, and the challenge to do better, rather than just doing the same things that they had done over past years. This project, though aimed at students' needs, ended up becoming a vehicle through which lecturers bought into the process of college improvement and affiliated with other lecturers with whom they shared common goals as teachers.

An unanticipated benefit of the peer tutoring programme was that, as the project progressed, colleges realised that student support services staff were not aware of the kind of academic support that their students needed because student support staff were not involved directly in curriculum and teaching activities. The peer tutoring programme and other CIP interventions demonstrated that academic support should be recognised as a dedicated function and resourced appropriately. The CIP also demonstrated how important it is that the student support services work with academic units to ensure that students are supported inside and outside the classroom.

Conclusion

The team commissioned to conduct an output-to-purpose review (OPR) of the CIP found evidence that the programme had managed to improve the capacity, functionality, and performance of the project colleges and, further, found evidence that the project was being institutionalised at all levels of the system, even in colleges with serious structural weaknesses. However, a series of caveats were put forward:

- First, recommendations included a refinement of the intervention and improvement of the approach, taking into consideration that the scope of the CIP was thought to be too wide given the resources available, including time.
- Second, the JET implementation team recognised that 'the turnaround process could not possibly be completed in the transition period, and that more medium- to long-term efforts would be required' (JET, 2012, cited in Scott, 2015: 19).
- Third, it was argued that to be sustainable, systemic changes require an enabling institutional environment. The project colleges in the Eastern Cape and Limpopo were at varying levels of institutional development and this affected the pace of change and the colleges' capacity to assimilate and sustain the intervention activities. Since conditions varied between colleges, the actions referred to above were not

- necessarily implemented with equal success in every site – whether main campus or satellite campus.
- Fourth, attention was drawn to the general levels of preparedness of new cohorts of students registering at different colleges each year. Depending on their catchment areas, the academic background of students registering at one college may differ substantially from those at another college in a different environment. In the drive to increase enrolments, colleges do not necessarily apply admissions criteria. There are no publicly set standard entry-level requirements for students to enter TVET colleges, or for any of the study programmes offered by the colleges. This means that students of widely differing abilities and aptitudes may be admitted for the same class. Graduation rates are affected by admissions policy, and there is evidence that directives regarding admissions contradict the need to improve graduation rates.

One of the objectives of the project was to establish the reasons behind the dysfunctionality of the colleges. The CIP successfully identified shortcomings and designed programmes to counteract dysfunctionality in the teaching and learning domain.

Nevertheless, to focus only on the teaching and learning function would not necessarily have served the purpose of the project. Therefore, the aims of the project included taking on conditions that had been created in previous incarnations of institutional change. The CIP was therefore obliged to deal with the baggage of previous experience, by, for example: fostering stability through settling outstanding issues affecting college functionality; securing strategic alignment of strategic and operational planning; supporting the foundations for good governance of each function; laying the foundations for enhanced performance in each functional area; strengthening all delivery functions in the college; and building a culture of performance.

In the interests of forging a strong TVET sector, the function of this book is to scrutinise assumptions about how to bring about change in the TVET college sector.

Chapter overview

The six chapters in this book are introduced to the reader in this short summary.

In Chapter 1, *Three decades of restructuring in further education colleges: Divergent outcomes across differing global vocational education and training systems*, Professor André Kraak, Centre for Research in Education and Labour (REAL), University of the Witwatersrand, adopts a historical and comparative international lens in approaching the FET/TVET institutional form from a global perspective. Though national systems of FET/TVET are widely divergent, Kraak draws upon particular national systems that he identifies as exemplars of two contrasting models of building TVET systems: a 'social solidarity' TVET system based on participative processes, as in the Netherlands; and a 'statist, prescriptive system of market-driven TVET', as in the United Kingdom. Analysis suggests that the former model is more successful than the latter. Based on these models, Kraak derives a set of axes according to which a national system of TVET may be plotted. Accordingly, in the social solidarity TVET system:

- Components in the TVET system are aligned;
- Processes are employer-led;
- Comprehensive reform in TVET system change is supported by industrial and labour market policies;
- Change in the TVET system is stable with elements of continuity; and
- Equitable access and growth of high-skill labour force is facilitated.

Based on conditions in the colleges of the Eastern Cape and Limpopo that participated in the CIP, there is evidence in the South African TVET system of poorly developed coordination and cooperation capabilities and disruptive change. In the presence of these macro-institutional conditions, to what degree would change management programmes such as the CIP have sufficient purchase to turn the participating colleges around?

In Chapter 2, *Unfinished business: Managing the transformation of FET colleges*, Dr Anthony Gewer, TVET consultant, addresses successive periods in the evolution of the FET (TVET) colleges up to the present. Gewer offers a periodised account of three phases in the transformation of the FET colleges system in South Arica since the advent of democracy. The early policy-oriented period saw colleges placed in the Department of Education rather than Labour which limited engagement with industry, and drew to a close with the promulgation of the 1998 FET Act (Act No. 98 of 1998). The Act located academic and vocational institutions alongside each other in the FET band, downplaying traditional distinctions between these institutional types. The second phase involved system-wide mergers and restructuring which combined enrolments and created opportunities to benefit from economies of scale, creating demand for new forms of management and relationships within colleges. The third phase involved extensive institutional recapitalisation, as well as 'recurriculation' via introduction of the NCV in 2007. This phase was characterised by consolidation of the colleges from the nine provincial departments of education into the DHET as part of establishing a coherent post-school institutional environment. Gewer argues that despite these advances, not enough has been done to address 'fundamental issues about the identity of the colleges, the curriculum they offer, or the role they are expected to play.' Government has sought 'to direct and drive transformation centrally, in the absence of a longer-term strategy, and this created mixed messages as to the policy trajectory for colleges.' These assertions are relevant to understanding the progress and impact of current institutional improvement projects such as the CIP that prompted the conception of this edited book.

In Chapter 3, the focus of this collection shifts from the broader landscape of institutional change and TVET college relationships with government and business, to internal relationships. Professor Ronel Blom, also of REAL, in her essay titled *Throwing good money after bad: The barriers South African vocational teachers experience in becoming competent educators*, identifies central challenges that college educators face. During the initiation phase of the CIP in 2011, rapid assessments of the status of the participating colleges were conducted, confirming that the central focus of the CIP should be on teaching and learning. Blom sets out to interrogate the non-subject matter barriers that confront TVET teachers in their efforts to achieve and retain their levels of competence and motivation to meet the academic and social needs of students. The five areas of concern identified include:

- The tremendous diversity and multiple levels of current TVET teacher qualifications which defy simple skills development or policy solutions and even contribute to 'capacity-building barriers';
- The effects of inequitable or insecure conditions of service that many TVET teachers have borne;
- Conditions of teaching at TVET colleges, including: rising student numbers; widening range in student ability; and limited introduction to new curricula;
- That TVET teachers have to cope with the sociological demands of alienated students, communities' lack of understanding of TVET, student learning difficulties, and students' difficulties in adapting to the college environment; and
- The TVET college funding model that encourages 'gaming' of the system to raise income and is a disincentive for articulation of programmes.

Blom argues that 'indiscriminate expansion in student enrolments is placing a huge burden on an already weak and poorly managed sector. The sheer pressure of student numbers will render policies ineffectual if concurrent improvements are not made in respect of TVET teachers themselves'. The author raises issues that bear relevance to the CIP project, many of which are linked to system policy issues external to the colleges. To what extent can programmes such as the CIP be expected to manage change successfully in a college 'from the inside out' when countervailing policy conditions 'from the outside in' are so powerful? Finally, embedded in the title of this contribution is the author's two-part plea: not to make poor investment decisions (the bad money) and not to waste more money pursuing the same or a similar course.

In Chapter 4, *A climate for change? Vertical and horizontal collegial relations in TVET colleges*, Professor Volker Wedekind and Zanele Buthelezi, once again from REAL, observe that hitherto minimal attention has been given to understanding the lived experience of lecturers in TVET colleges. They cite arguments from the literature that 'positive collegial relations enhance the possibilities for professional development … and contribute to the development of the organisation as a whole' (Wedekind, 2001). Yet their research based on a qualitative methodology strongly suggests that 'collegial relations, both horizontal and vertical, are generally poor or problematic'. Intergenerational, gender, seniority, race and occupational specialisation or the 'division of labour' relationships with management in colleges are implicated. There is little evidence that lecturers consistently practise modalities through which collegial relations are developed or strengthened, such as mentoring, peer coaching, collaboration, partnerships, team work and professional development. Lecturers express antipathy toward their college's central office management and council; and dissatisfaction with government policy which is perceived as contributing to systemic and institutional challenges. A disjuncture between centralisation of managerial/bureaucratic power and uncertain lecturer employment status prevails on some campuses. The authors explore and interpret underlying narratives, some of which depict deep-rooted relations of distrust.

In a slack labour market characterised by low or slow growth and poor demand for labour, how graduates transition into work can present a serious bottleneck that frustrates and damages their future expectations. Colleges are adopting programmes to facilitate this transition. In Chapter 5, *Preparing TVET college graduates for the workplace: Employers' views,* Professor Joy Papier, Seamus Needham, Nigel Prinsloo and Timothy McBride of the Institute for Post-School Studies, University of the Western Cape, focus on employers' expectations of college students and graduates from training programmes in the Tourism and Hospitality, Engineering, and Wholesale and Retail industries for which colleges traditionally offer training. Employers' perspectives were elicited about their knowledge of and interactions with TVET college graduates seeking work in their respective sectors. In addition, the study explored perceptions of employers regarding the employability of college graduates. Employers averred that graduates needed training in:

- Being professional, for example appearance, work ethic;
- Communication, for example customer relations;
- Understanding the workplace, for example rights and responsibilities;
- Values and ethics, for example honesty; and
- Application of college learning to the workplace, for example preparedness to put skills into practice and engage with workplace social relations.

Elements of the skills deemed by respondents as missing in graduates were found to exist across the N4–N6 courses in the National Accredited Technical Education Diploma (NATED) syllabus. Lecturers addressed the desired skills but not in a systematic way for explicit workplace preparation. Based on employer recommendations, a prototype 'workplace preparation programme' as a supplement to the N6 programme has been designed and implementation is being monitored with a view to assessing impact. Firms viewed work placement as an opportunity for both parties – employer and graduate – to evaluate each other's potential for a mutually beneficial contracted relationship. Respondents argued in favour of closer relationships between industry and colleges around work placement, taking the position 'that companies should be involved sooner rather than later'.

In the concluding piece, Chapter 6, *What will it take to turn TVET colleges around? Evaluation of a large-scale college improvement programme,* Carmel Marock, Independent Research Consultant specialising in skills and education, Eleanor Hazell, Monitoring and Evaluation (M&E) Manager, JET Education Services, and Bina Akoobhai, formerly Specialist Manager, JET Education Services, offer the opportunity to consider how the CIP, a large-scale and relatively long-duration intervention programme, impacted the TVET colleges. This chapter addresses the complex parallel processes of implementation and institutional response. In reading the final offering in this collection, the reader has the advantage of being able to browse the preceding chapters for more contextual detail as needed. Carmel Marock and Eleanor Hazell view the CIP through a monitoring and evaluation lens and bring to the table learnings from the M&E process which drew on different data sources and methods including developing a logic model: an initial rapid assessment, in-depth case studies, documentary analysis and interviews as well as baseline, formative and summative evaluations. The M&E programme addressed core intervention-specific questions such as: What did the CIP produce, deliver, and achieve in the context of what challenges and impediments? As importantly, the M&E process raised the following three critical questions: Which challenges could a programme such as the CIP be expected to address with reasonable expectations of positive impact? What needs to be in place for such a project to succeed? And: what needs to be in place to support sustainability? In the course of the CIP, a strategic decision was made to focus in particular on teaching and learning, which included capacitating college lecturers, as the key theme. Effectively the aspiration of a 'college turnaround' was set aside, though expectations remained high. The analysis suggests that the key to sustaining newly acquired practices lies in the capacity of the DHET to support a closer working relationship with colleges.

References

Department of Higher Education and Training (DHET). (2013). *White paper for post-school education and training: Building an expanded, effective and integrated post-school system.* Pretoria: Department of Higher Education and Training.

Finance and Fiscal Commission. (2013). Funding of the South African Further Education and Training Sector. In: *Submission for the division of revenue (budget proposals) 2014/2015.* Pretoria: Finance and Fiscal Commission. Chapter 3, Table 7: Participation of 19–24 year olds in FET college education per province – 2011, p. 39. [Available at http://www.ffc.co.za/index.php/2-uncategorised/90-chapters-2014-15, Accessed 04 December 2015].

Scott, G. & Associates. (2015). *Inception report (April) for the summative evaluation of the JET Education Services Technical and Vocational Education Colleges Improvement Project funded under the NSF: DHET Capacity Development and Support Grant.* Unpublished report.

Republic of South Africa (RSA). (2012). *Further Education and Training Colleges Amendment Act, No. 3 of 2012.* Pretoria: Government Printer.

Statistics South Africa. (2013). *Millennium Development Goals – Goal 2: Achieve universal primary education.* Pretoria: Statistics South Africa, Figure 9, education by gender, p. 26.

Wedekind, V. (2001). A figurational analysis of the lives and careers of some South African teachers. Doctoral thesis submitted to the University of Manchester.

chapter 1

THREE DECADES OF RESTRUCTURING IN FURTHER EDUCATION COLLEGES
DIVERGENT OUTCOMES ACROSS DIFFERING GLOBAL VOCATIONAL EDUCATION AND TRAINING SYSTEMS

Professor André Kraak
Centre for Research in Education and Labour (REAL),
University of the Witwatersrand

Introduction

This chapter provides an overview of institutional change within the further education (FE) college sector globally. This is a massive task, and the analysis highlights only those global shifts that have resonance with the South African context. What is clear, firstly, is that almost all college systems across the globe have faced similar institutional pressures and dramatic restructuring. Secondly, the outcomes of these pressures and changes – mergers, the intensification of work through the introduction of performance indicators and targets, and pressures for institutions to self-fund a significant portion of their cost structure – have been highly divergent. The discussion in this chapter presents an ideal-type of two dominant institutional outcomes:

- The first is the Anglo-Saxon response, ironically from the region which pioneered most of the reforms associated with 'neo-liberal' institutional change, but which has fared worst under the changes. This has happened because of the weakening of the 'fit' or alignment between the college sector on the supply side and the skill requirements of employers on the demand side. The continuous and erratic nature of this restructuring over three decades has created an environment of relentless institutional instability. New public management (NPM) reforms, obsessed with 'performativity' and the meeting of annual 'targets', has led to a culture of minimal compliance, informal defiance, and outright resistance.
- The second response is the 'continental European' and 'developmental state' response, which comprises the continuation and strengthening of the institutional alignment between the demand and supply sides of the national economies involved. Countries such as the Netherlands, Finland, and Singapore have (in very different ways) seen a significant strengthening of their FE college sectors, and a ramping up of the skills of the national workforce during this period – the same period in which certain Anglo-Saxon countries faced major institutional instability, uncertainty, and weakening.

This ideal-type risks over-generalising the conditions in all of the countries located in these two camps, but does highlight the institutional trajectory traversed by countries such as the United Kingdom (UK) and South Africa over the past three decades – a period of immense institutional change, pressure, and decline (not improvement) – versus the success of reforms in the Netherlands and Singapore (the former typical of the 'continental European', the latter typical of the Asian 'development state' routes). In these countries, changes in the college sector have underpinned improvements in global economic competitiveness, and this alignment on the demand side is the crucial 'ideal-type' difference between the Anglo-Saxon and other technical and vocational education and training (TVET) models.

The discussion of FE colleges cannot start without a look at the wider education and training (ET) system within which the colleges 'fit'. Indeed, the alignment of the differing sub-components of the wider ET system is a critically important differentiating factor in the international literature and allows us to distinguish between differing national TVET systems globally. Key 'alignment' interactions include links with employers, sector skills councils (SSCs), and higher education. Building on the work of the 'variety of capitalism' and 'high-skills' literatures (see Hall & Soskice, 2001; Hall & Thelen, 2007; Green, Mostafa & Preston, 2010; see also Ashton & Green, 1996; and Brown, Green & Lauder, 2001), it is argued here that there are at least four differing ideal-type TVET institutional arrangements globally, and that these four types of systems have survived the restructuring of the 1980s and 1990s very differently. These systems and their core characteristics are represented in Table 2 on the next page.

This chapter will focus on the key differences between two of these TVET models, the 'social solidarity' TVET model of the Netherlands and the 'statist' model of the UK's TVET system, and the manner in which the college sector in particular has coped with three decades of neo-liberal restructuring. The analysis will conclude by identifying what is similar and different in the way in which the South African college sector has been reformed since the advent of democracy in 1994.

Historical evolution of neo-liberal restructuring

A second important observation is required before we discuss reforms in the FE college sector. We first need to understand the dramatic changes imposed on the public sector (including the public TVET system) in most countries in the 1980s and 1990s, commonly understood as the era of neo-liberalism. The neo-liberal reformist thrust arose most forcefully in the United States of America (USA) and the UK under the leadership of Margaret Thatcher and Ronald Reagan in the late 1970s and early 1980s, and was a response to the acute economic crisis of the time. The oil price shocks of 1973 and 1979 saw profits shrink whilst wages grew. There was a massive investment slump. Taken together, all of these conditions resulted in the dual crises of high levels of inflation and unemployment. The inability of social democratic governments to deal effectively with the growing crisis was blamed on the 'rigidities' thrown up by the post-war Keynesian welfare state. By the 1990s, neo-liberalism was established as the dominant discourse of policy reform globally. Its basic tenets were:

- The most successful economies in the world economic system are those based on free market principles.
- Free market forces function optimally when unconstrained by institutional or legislative interference. The laws of demand and supply are considered the supreme regulatory mechanisms in the economy.
- Typically, the neo-liberal position requires a reduction in the powers of the state in the market place and the exclusion of other interest groups (such as trade unions) who would otherwise interfere with the natural functioning of the free market.
- In short, the remedy proposed by neo-liberal economists has, in most cases, been a bitter pill to swallow: it has entailed the deregulation of the labour market (abolition of minimum wages and job protection), the dismemberment of labour market institutions (the decline of central bargaining and wage determination structures), and the liberalisation of international trade (via the withdrawal of tariff protection and the subsidisation of local industries) (Harvey, 2005; Castells, 1996).

TABLE 2 Divergent national systems of post-school provision

Type of system	Countries	Types of college	Key characteristics
The 'social solidarity' model	Netherlands	Regional occupational colleges (ROCs)	• Regional colleges started in 1996 from the merger of several fragmented vocational institutes and colleges • Colleges closely aligned to industry needs through industrial bargaining system • Demand-led colleges • High progression from colleges to applied universities • Very effective sector skills council system put in place in 1996 • Adopted national qualification framework (NQF) and outcomes-based education (OBE) models which act to hold the entire TVET system together
	Finland and Republic of Ireland	Strengthened school vocational route	• Improved pathways from vocational school stream into newly created or merged Institutes of Technology (polytechnics)
The 'development state' model	Singapore	Institute of Technology with three campuses (not a polytechnic, more a mega-college institution)	• The state very successful in restructuring TVET to meet industrial policy needs across a number of long-wave 'ramping-up' policy phases
The 'market' model	USA	Community colleges linked to Local Workforce Investment Boards (LWIBs)	• Strong link at local and regional level with LWIBs • Successful interventions to upgrade employed workforce using community colleges
	Brazil	Effective 'S-system' institutions managed by employers since 1949	• Employer driven • Comprise sector-based post-school vocational institutes • State has no strong public college system
The 'statist' model – highly prescriptive	United Kingdom	Further education colleges	• Supply-side driven • No employer buy-in and participation • State is highly prescriptive on how the system should work • Status of vocational qualifications in the labour market extremely poor

Since the 1980s, and particularly after the collapse of the socialist-command eco-nomies of the former Soviet Bloc territories in the early 1990s, this economic wisdom has attained a powerful hegemony throughout the capitalist world. Neo-liberal economics is now the accepted orthodoxy of governments across the globe.

Implications for post-school education

A key part of the neo-liberal package of reforms which swept the capitalist world from the 1980s onwards were those reforms destined for the public sector. The new techniques of public administration, termed 'New Public Management' (NPM), were introduced on a wide scale in the late 1980s and throughout the 1990s as a counter to the limitations of the traditional Weberian bureaucracies that had been previously dominant. NPM argued for more market-oriented approaches to public administration. O'Flynn (2007) argues that much of the NPM restructuring was heavily influenced by 'public choice theory', which held that 'governments were unresponsive, inefficient and monopolistic' (2007: 355). In this view, politicians and civil servants acted in pursuit of self-interest and not efficiency, and as a consequence, bureaucracies led to massive resource wastage. What was required, argued the NPM doctrine, were competitive markets for public services (O'Flynn, 2007: 355). O'Flynn highlights four of NPM's foundational principles:

1. The introduction of explicit standards and measures of performance;
2. Greater emphasis on output controls;
3. Greater competition in the public sector; and
4. The introduction of private sector styles of management practice (O'Flynn, 2007: 354).

The biggest and most destructive change introduced into the public sector – impacting also the public TVET system – was the obsession with establishing performance indicators and targets for each line of public sector work. Payne and Keep (2011) believe the impact of NPM on TVET policy has been huge, contributing to today's 'top-down' and highly centralised approach to TVET governance:

> *Essentially, the government set targets in terms of the proportion of the workforce expected to hold qualifications at various levels and then directed funding accordingly. These targets, which were arrived at without meaningful consultation, reflected the Government's view of what constituted legitimate 'training' or 'learning' and what, in its mind, the state, employers and learners ought together to be aspiring towards. Supporting this was a complex infrastructure of multi-level planning mechanisms, designed to match skills supply and demand (from both learners and employers), together with top-down interventionist forms of performance management and control to ensure the responsiveness of colleges and other providers. (Payne & Keep, 2011: 4)*

Keep and James (2012) argue that the problem with this approach to TVET policy is its misdiagnosis of the underlying economic problems facing the UK – which they argue are fundamentally about the low demand from employers for higher level skills. It is this demand-side issue that needs to be addressed – through interventions that reshape employers' needs for higher-level skills, work re-organisation, and the better utilisation of newly acquired skills in the workforce. Coercive performance regimes do not help.

This obsession with supply-side interventions – over more than three decades – is held alongside the naive belief that low-skill jobs will disappear if workers are better educated. On the contrary, low-skill jobs have persisted into the current era even whilst the workforce becomes more educated. Keep and James argue that there is a set of mutually reinforcing factors that reduces the incentives acting on individuals and employers to participate and invest in education and training. Acting in concert, all of these negative factors inhibit the impetus for employers to want to increase the levels of education and training or change the nature of precarious and low-skill 'bad jobs' (Keep & James, 2012: 211).

Vocational education and training reform in the United Kingdom

Even though the Conservative Party in the 1980s under Thatcher sought to deregulate and diminish the size and impact of the state in the market economy, it is ironic that the new policy levers and the many new parastatal bodies set up to regulate TVET meant an increase in state micro-management and bureaucracy and a steep increase in the transactional costs entailed in undertaking enterprise training (Steer *et al*, 2007: 1). This micro-management has been continuous across the differing political administrations since the early 1980s. Successive governments adopted the same misguided diagnosis of the UK's socioeconomic woes – that a concentration on the supply side of education would solve most of society's ills (Keep & James, 2012: 222; Payne & Keep, 2011: 1).

The decisive reform during the Thatcherite era was the 1992 Higher and Further Education Act. Under this Act, which led to the replacement of state provision with competitive semi-independent college providers, a process generally referred to as the 'incorporation of colleges' took place (Boocock, 2013: 309). Colleges were shifted away from local authority control to autonomous college 'business units', controlled financially by a series of state entities such as the Further Education Funding Council, the Learning and Skills Council (LSC), and, more recently, the Skills Funding Agency (SFA).

New Labour, 1997–2010

New Labour's restructuring efforts have undoubtedly made the strongest impact on TVET in the UK. According to Payne and Keep, New Labour's skills strategy rested upon three fundamental assumptions. Firstly, New Labour held an unshakeable belief in supply-side interventions and neglect of the demand side. This educational policy imperative was strengthened by the absence of any real industrial policy to move employers up the value chain towards higher value added and higher levels of productivity. The economic status quo was left untouched, with primacy given to increasing educational outputs. Secondly, the New Labour government believed that a focus on improving the education levels of lowly skilled adults and unemployed youth would allow these groups to move off welfare, enter employment, and progress in the labour market, thereby contributing to the government's agenda around social inclusion.

And lastly, New Labour believed that a significant investment by the state in TVET would provide a public subsidy that could 'leverage' employer 'buy-in' and investment in skills (Payne & Keep, 2011: 4–5).

The Coalition Government and its TVET policies, 2010–2015

The Coalition Government, led by the Conservative Party from 2010 to 2015, introduced large budget cuts which affected the higher and further education sectors severely. For example, the budget for further education was reduced by 25% from £4.3 billion to £3.2 billion during 2014–15 (Payne & Keep, 2011: 8). These cuts affected all of the former Labour Government's programmes discussed earlier – many of them were terminated. For example, the Coalition Government scrapped all public funding for those over the age of 24 studying toward Level 3 national vocational qualifications (NVQs) and ended the entitlement for people over the age of 25 to take a first Level 2 qualification free of charge.

The Coalition Government was also opposed to what it considered Labour's 'culture of bureaucratic central planning and regulatory control', its obsession with targeting and performance measurement, and with learners and colleges chasing the money rather than attending to the real demand-side needs of employers (Payne & Keep, 2011: 10).

Apart from these budget cuts, commentators argue that there are many continuities in TVET policy. The wider education and training framework is 'still broadly congruent with the global trajectory of Neo-Liberalism' (Fisher & Simmons, 2012: 32; see also Steedman, 2011: 2, 4). Payne and Keep (2011) argue that the Coalition Government is still committed to the view that sees skills supply as the central policy lever for delivering both economic performance and social mobility (Payne & Keep, 2011: 9).

The schooling system

The UK has a devolved system of governance for education and training, with differences between the systems for Scotland, Northern Ireland, Wales, and England. Scotland, in particular, has an education system with a long history of independence from other parts of the UK, and this has intensified with the drive towards devolution. This chapter will focus primarily on national training policy, and therefore will use the descriptor 'UK' to signify this, knowing well that there are significant policy differences with regard to Scotland – much of which is not within the ambit of this discussion.

Schooling is compulsory from age 5 to 16. The national curriculum comprises different compulsory subjects, with subjects like English, Mathematics, Science and ICT serving as the core curricula. At age 16 most pupils take public examinations for the General Certificate of Secondary Education (GCSE), which is pegged at NQF Level 2 in the UK's system (Cuddy & Leney, 2005: 23).

After completion of compulsory education, school students may choose between a general (academic) or vocational track, or follow a mixture of the two routes. Normally, the upper secondary phase lasts two years, from age 16 to 18. The final qualification received is the General Senior Certificate of Education (GSCE) A-levels (Level 3 on the NVQ) – equivalent to South Africa's matriculation certificate with exemption to enter higher education.

A-levels are elective single-subject qualifications. Students are encouraged to study up to five subjects in the first year of post-secondary education and upon completion are awarded the GSCE advanced subsidiary (AS) qualification. Those who continue in the second year study more demanding units in three of these five subjects to obtain the full GSCE (A levels) which is pegged at Level 3 (Cuddy & Leney, 2005: 23). These school phases are illustrated in Figure 2.

FIGURE 2 Simplified overview of the NQF in the United Kingdom

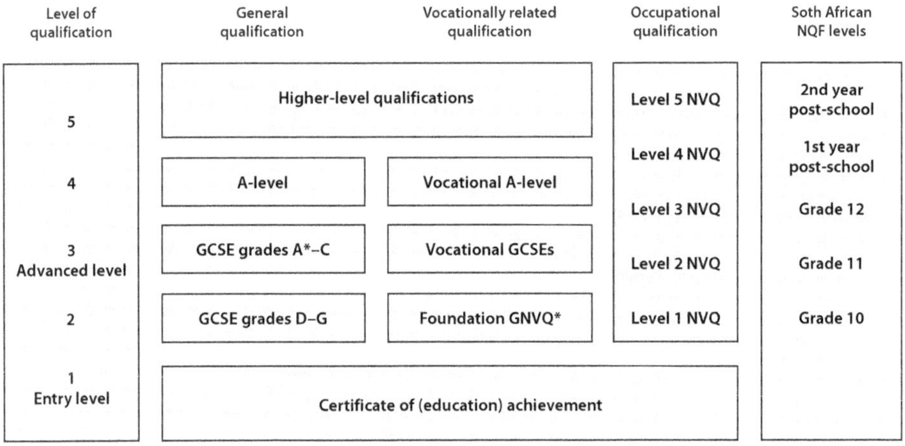

Level of qualification	General qualification	Vocationally related qualification	Occupational qualification	Soth African NQF levels
5	Higher-level qualifications		Level 5 NVQ	2nd year post-school
4	A-level	Vocational A-level	Level 4 NVQ	1st year post-school
			Level 3 NVQ	Grade 12
3 Advanced level	GCSE grades A*–C	Vocational GCSEs	Level 2 NVQ	Grade 11
2	GCSE grades D–G	Foundation GNVQ*	Level 1 NVQ	Grade 10
1 Entry level	Certificate of (education) achievement			

Source: Cuddy & Leney (2005: 25).

In addition to the academic route highlighted in Figure 2, there is a vocational progression route. For example, vocational GCSEs are available in eight subjects: Applied Science, Applied Information Technology (IT), Applied Business, Applied Art and Design, Engineering, Manufacturing, Health and Social Care, and Leisure and Tourism (Cuddy & Leney, 2005: 27).

Compared to other industrialised countries, learners' attainment at the GCSE level by the age of 16 is good, but staying-on rates after the age of 16 (Level 2 and 3 qualifications) are poor. Consequently, the proportion of the population having skills, particularly at Level 3, is lower in the UK than in other industrialised countries. For the UK as a whole, a major policy concern is that approximately 10% of school leavers at age 16 do not enter employment, further education, or training. Without further government intervention they are at risk of remaining permanently unemployed and socially excluded (Cuddy & Leney, 2005: 13).

Table 3 highlights the low retention rates of learners in the schooling system after compulsory education ends at age 16. In 2003, only 72% of students continued with schooling, 11% left school and enrolled for vocational training, 8% found employment, and 5% were unemployed. However, there are significant regional variations in the UK, with unemployment in Scotland reaching 16% in 2003 (Cuddy & Leney, 2005: 14).

TABLE 3 Destination of school leavers in the United Kingdom, 1991–2003

	England	Wales	Northern Ireland	Scotland
Number of school leavers (thousands)	608.0	37.7	26.3	57.3
of which (%)				
Education	72	74	70	52
Government support training*	7	8	19	5
Employment	11	7	5	23
Unemployment/not available for work	8	6	2	16
Unknown or left area	4	5	4	4

Source: Cuddy & Leney (2005: 28).

Proliferation of NVQs

NVQs were introduced into the UK TVET system in the early 1990s, intended only for the post-16 school phase. However, a range of NVQs were offered at Levels 1 and 2. At Level 3 (the culmination of the 12-year schooling phase), the range of subject choice and specialisation offered is wide, and a number of UK students, usually in the 16 to 18 age group, choose a vocational route in the final phase of schooling. Students studying for A levels and for the 'sixth form' pathway into higher education constitute by far the largest single group moving out of upper secondary school. A second pathway through upper secondary education is enrolment in full-time, non-A-level courses, most of which are 'Level 3' Business and Technology Education Council (BTEC) awards. These BTEC awards differ markedly from A levels in that they all have a more or less specific vocational orientation. They are, nonetheless, well recognised by higher education and widely accepted for entry into degree courses, especially in similar vocational areas. This is not the case with the third pathway through secondary schooling – as illustrated in Table 4. While 40% of students follow the first pathway on route to higher education, and 18% follow the second pathway, taking advanced craft or BTEC Level 3 courses with clear progression value as discussed above, the third group, comprising those who graduate with only Level 1 or 2 programmes, is large at 30% (Wolf, 2011: 51). This is a major skills deficit at the heart of the entire UK education model.

Further education colleges

The UK history of FE colleges and their insertion within the wider TVET system is distinctive in the international literature – this is so because of the strong sense of inferiority and failure associated with the college sector historically. Much of this vocational pessimism has roots in a deeply entrenched set of class, ideological, and

TABLE 4 Study programmes of 16–18-year-olds in educational institutions

Pathway to higher education	Qualification	Percentage of the 16 to 18 age group
1. Academic route	A levels only (3+) – the academic route	33%
	1 or 2 A levels plus other qualifications	7%
2. Vocational academic route	No A levels, but at least one Level 3 course of study. Most of these (85%) are for BTEC awards	18%
3. No access to higher education	Level 2 or Level 1 or below Level 1	30%

Source: Wolf (2011: 47).

institutional prejudices against the value and prestige of vocational education (Fisher & Simmons, 2012: 31). This antipathy for the vocational has spilled over into the labour market, where graduates with vocational qualifications are not guaranteed high levels of employability and earnings potential – as is the case in the Central and Northern European collective TVET systems of Germany, Netherlands and Denmark (Fisher & Simmons, 2012: 31). All of this history has rubbed off on the institutional image of FE colleges, which are the main conduits for vocational education in the UK.

FE colleges in the UK, in their early history, were under-funded and relatively insignificant. They started as mechanics institutes and centres for adult technical education and began receiving funding from local municipalities only in 1944. However, by the 1980s, the numbers and sizes of FE colleges had grown so fast that government began to merge them into larger polytechnics. By 1992, significant academic drift had occurred, with many higher education programmes being offered in colleges, leading to 30 polytechnics becoming 'new' universities.

Alongside this drift into higher education, the FE sector underwent major reform, the most significant of which was to remove FE colleges from local municipality control and to steer them into highly marketised relations with employers and learners. As indicated earlier, this represented the height of Thatcherite neo-liberal restructuring in the FE sector. Significant dissatisfaction with these changes prevailed in the sector throughout the 1990s and 2000s.

Lack of employer buy-in

The most vocal and repeated of all criticisms of the TVET system in the UK is the claim of limited employer 'buy-in'. For example, in an important review of employer voice in the UK Sector Skills Councils, the United Kingdom Commission on Employment and Skills (UKCES) noted that there is a mismatch of expectations between employers, public sector partners, and government about what employers are being asked to do. Employers are frustrated. They expect to see a return on their investment of time – the kind of impact that translates into business benefits (UKCES, 2010: 3).

Payne (2007) argues that historically weak British employer associations are part of the problem, made worse by the collapse of multi-employer, industry-level collective bargaining in the United Kingdom – a development entirely due to neo-liberal reforms since the 1980s (Payne, 2007: 10–11). In the current context, Lanning and Lawton (2012) note a 'cultural resistance to social partnership among many employer representative bodies' in the UK (Lanning & Lawton, 2012: 37).

Statist models

In contrast to employer-led approaches, the system which has evolved in the UK (and South Africa) is civil servant dominated, with government imposing national skills policy frameworks on employers and FE colleges without their consent and buy-in. The UKCES states this contradictory reality bluntly: 'the public sector is the main driver behind some "employer-led" arrangements so the idea of employer leadership is a misnomer' (2010: 16). Lanning and Lawton (2012: 3) agree and argue that the failure to engage employers has led to an over-reliance on centralised state-led programmes and institutions to fill the gap.

Ashton (2006) argues that the remit of the SSCs and FE colleges is not to represent and reflect employers' skill needs, but to respond to the national policy agenda of government. He provides an example of the *Train to Gain* campaign implemented during the Blair administration. Employers sought training of new entrants at Level 3 on the NQF (matric equivalent), but government policy was to deliver opportunities at Level 2 (assisting disadvantaged workers to complete a secondary school certificate). Employers lost out and were only able to train Level 2 trainees using government money (Ashton, 2006: 7, 10).

Targeting

The establishment of targets in the UK system has also had negative effects. Targets are generally national in orientation and are not sufficiently calibrated to take regional or sectoral differences into account. Targets therefore have the effect of imposing 'one-size-fits-all' solutions onto all sectors. Secondly, targets also tend to encourage FE colleges to opt for the quickest, easiest, and cheapest routes to meeting quantitative targets – irrespective of real demand-side need.

Targets imposed in the college sector included the introduction of LSC success rates, focused on the achievement of 16 to 18 and 19+ student groupings. These success rates had to be achieved above the benchmark (national average) if a college was to achieve Centre of Vocational Excellence (COVE) status from the LSC and attain a 'good' grade within the Ofsted inspection process (Boocock, 2013: 310).

Rise of managerialism

These institutional changes stimulated the growth of a new cadre of managers whose job it was to ensure the attainment of these targets, benchmarks, and indicators. The changes also stimulated competition between colleges, and, most importantly, a rapid growth and spread of managerialism across the sector (Mather, Worrall & Mather, 2012: 537).

In detailed research cases studies, Boocock (2013) and Mather *et al* (2012) both show that middle management and most lecturers in the college sector saw these changes as the imposition of an 'authoritarian political' style in which 'debate and discussion were closed down – a style contrasting markedly with the pre-2000 distributed leadership arrangements' (Boocock, 2013: 313).

Restructuring also entailed curriculum reform and tighter control of the labour process of lecturers. Curriculum reform was justified on the basis of developing a more 'customer and outward focused' syllabus. Curriculum areas have been reorganised several times since the early 2000s, creating demotivated lecturers. As Mather *et al* suggest in their college case studies, there were also continual attempts to restructure lecturers' timetables in order to change lecturers' job content. Some lecturers had been told to assume responsibility for work-based vocational courses which conflicted with both their subject specialisms and their previous college-based roles. Senior managers presented this as a need for more flexibility. They asserted that vocational courses are 'assessor driven and not lecturer driven' (Mather *et al*, 2012: 541). Mather *et al* see this continual revisiting of curricula, staff timetabling, and lecturer contracts as

> *enabling the tighter management of lecturers' time and activities. We argue that this level of scrutiny over what lecturers actually do runs counter to notions of 'can-do' and 'empowering' cultures that senior managers purported to espouse. We felt we had uncovered managerial double-speak where their rhetoric about empowerment was designed to cloak the continual disempowerment of lecturers as the locus of control shifted from the professional to a cadre of senior managers.* (Mather et al, 2012: 542)

Mather *et al* argue that NPM has had the effect of cheapening and degrading labour through its role in facilitating management control. This has affected workers' experiences of work, as 'the locus of control over the pace and nature of jobs has become increasingly contested' (Mather *et al*, 2012: 535). Ball (2012) concurs and indicates that these NPM techniques involve 'the subordination of moral obligations to economic ones'. In Ball's view, 'economically productive individuals' are the central resource in a reformed, entrepreneurial public sector. Those who 'under-perform are subject to moral approbation' (Ball, 2012: 20).

Threat of job loss

Another feature of the restructuring process has been to change employment relations, to the detriment of staff. Often done under the guise of a curriculum review, permanently appointed staff have had to re-apply for their restructured jobs, with many facing redundancy. New staff have come in on contracts without the employment benefits of the previous era (Mather *et al*, 2012: 543). These employment changes severely damaged the professional confidence of FE college staff, and the constant pressure to perform, to excel, has created very high levels of both institutional and individual anxiety (Boocock, 2013: 319).

Cultural change

Much of the thrust of neo-liberal restructuring has been more about ideological principles and less about organisational effectiveness. This is explicit when examining the rise of excessive managerialism in the FE college sector. Mather *et al* point to the increased role of senior managers in the college sector who have attempted to realign employees' attitudes through multi-layered processes of organisational change. This process usually involves culture change initiatives, often led by external consultants. As a result, new groups of managers have been created to espouse corporate values and the idea of a more 'flexible, responsive, consumer-focused and forward-looking college' (Mather *et al*, 2012: 535–536).

These senior managers have a preoccupation with the cultivation of certain cultural norms, creating corporate cultures, identifying 'good lecturers', and tackling 'laggards'. According to Mather *et al*, lecturers felt that they had to behave in particular ways while at work and in ways that suggested surface compliance and the suppression of overt resistance. Drawing on Ball (2003), these writers argue that in their case studies of FE colleges, senior management aims were the same – to reduce resistance to change at the chalk face. In this process of attempting cultural and ideological control, lecturers were not unquestioning and not entirely compliant, as we will see in a later section.

This obsessive pursuit of targets led to the labelling of this period of UK education history as one of 'performativity' (Ball, 2012). Performativity implies the realignment and re-education of lecturers and their immediate managers to accept and conform to new ways of working, behaving, and thinking. What this means in practice is that lecturers are expected to perform in prescribed ways, as defined by a dominant managerial discourse (Mather *et al*, 2012: 535). Ball describes the devastating effect this performativity has on professional ethics and curriculum delivery:

> *The first order effect of performativity is to re-orient pedagogical and scholarly activities towards those which are likely to have a positive impact on measurable performance outcomes and are a deflection of attention away from aspects of social, emotional or moral development that have no immediate measurable performative value. Teachers' judgments about class or lecture room processes may thus be subverted and superceded by the demands of measurement or at the very least a new set of dilemmas is produced which set the tyranny of metrics over and against professional judgment. (Ball, 2012: 20)*

Resistance

Did FE college staff in the UK resist these changes, or did they become compliant, docile, and deprofessionalised workers? Mather *et al* suggest that these reforms produced a 'world of surface compliance underlain by cynicism, alienation and disbelief' (Mather *et al*, 2012: 540). Leathwood and Read (2013: 1168) and Ball (2012: 17), writing about similar neo-liberal restructuring in higher education, argue that most staff surrendered to compliance, especially with the demands of performativity, and in so doing became 'complicit' in its implementation. However, middle managers and lecturing staff did resist in many covert forms, mostly at the micro-institutional level. Page (2011) presents findings from a study of first-tier managers in a number of FE colleges. He discovers a range of resistant behaviours along a continuum, from overt acts such as principled dissent to covert acts such as cutting corners and cognitive escape (Page, 2011: 1). Another more covert act of resistance was that of 'institutional forgetfulness' or 'organisational amnesia'. This took the form of not responding to the endless requests for performativity-related information and reports. These requests were so frequent and so repetitive that, if ignored, Page argues, few non-submissions were ever followed up. Those making these requests appeared to forget they had made the request in the first place. Also, when reports were submitted, they appeared to descend into a 'black hole' and were never mentioned again (Page, 2011: 6).

Another activity of resistance was to 'cut corners' – what Page sees as employees' attempts to 're-appropriate control over their work' (2011: 7). Boocock calls some of this activity 'gaming' – which he describes as a means of improving success rates. Specific gaming activities include 'cream skimming' (selecting more able pupils), 'parking' less able students (providing such students with little support), offering extra support to 'marginal students', 'constructive' exclusion through pressure on students to leave voluntarily, and removing weak students from harder courses by putting them onto easier NVQ equivalents (Boocock, 2013: 311). All of these gaming activities – essentially 'cheating' the system – are the unintended consequences of policy reforms designed by UK politicians and civil servants who never foresaw such negative outcomes.

The post-school system in the Netherlands

Post-school restructuring in the Netherlands provides a sharp contrast to the experience of institutional reforms in the UK. This comparison provides a best-practice template for educational change occurring under challenging circumstances. The Netherlands TVET system stands out because of the stability and consensus it achieved during the restructuring period – which comprised many of the same instruments so damaging in the UK context, including college mergers, the imposition of performance management, and the adoption of national qualification frameworks and outcomes based education. More importantly, the educational reforms introduced in the Netherlands since 1996 strengthened the education system's alignment with changing industry needs. The primary factor contributing to all of this success was the corporatist Dutch industrial relations system which ensured a smooth transition to the new post-school model, based on trust and buy-in from employers and unions.

History of Dutch vocational education and training

Technical and vocational schools were started relatively late in the Netherlands – they began only in 1919 – compared with the German model. These late evolutionary steps led to the establishment of an apprenticeship system which was significantly smaller than the model evolving in neighbouring Germany (Geurts & Meijers, 2009: 1). An important development in the Dutch model occurred in 1968 with the 'Mammoetwet' or Mammoth Act, which consolidated the vocational pathway through the entire senior secondary phase. This legislation positioned general and vocational education as equal alternatives alongside one another, with the possibility of reciprocal transfers (Visser, 2010: 11). Higher professional education was catered for in a separate Act in 1986, which allowed for the establishment of tertiary TVET in the form of applied/polytechnic institutions of higher education (Visser, 2010: 3).

However, the main development in the growth of the Dutch post-school vocational system came with the passing of the Wet Educatie en Beroepsonderwijs (WEB) Act in 1996. This Adult and Vocational Education Act put in place the institutional architecture which today so successfully drives the Dutch TVET system. The main aim of the 1996 WEB Act was to devise a set of interactions between institutions which would ensure far more effective 'system alignment' and complementarity than was the case previously (Sung, 2010: 21). The new elements that were introduced alongside existing institutions that were consolidated and merged included:

1. A 'dual' system of secondary school with one track for general academic schooling and another for vocational education and training: these two routes are treated as equal in the education sphere and in the labour market.
2. A system of 17 sectoral bodies called 'Knowledge Centres' (Kenniscentra) established along the line of broad economic sectors: the Knowledge Centres play a crucial role as the 'starting point' for the design of national vocational qualifications (Sung, 2010: 21).
3. The creation of 43 regional training colleges (ROCs) formed out of the merger of hundreds of local training colleges: these colleges manage the 'school-based' learning of senior secondary vocational education. All students (work or school based) follow the same qualifications that are designed by the Knowledge Centres.

The vocational post-school sector

The Dutch senior secondary vocational education track has three levels: it starts in junior secondary school as 'preparatory vocational education' (VMBO), it continues after compulsory schooling at age 16 in senior secondary school as 'secondary vocational education' (MBO), and it peaks in post-school education as 'professional higher education' (HBO) – applied or polytechnic higher education. The system starts at a very early age, with Dutch children having to make their first educational choice at the age of 12 – whether to continue with general (academic) schooling or follow the preparatory vocational route. Those with lower results academically tend to choose the vocational route. The system is flexible though and allows children to move back to academic schooling after a foundation year in vocational education if they so choose (Reubzaet, Romme & Geerstma, 2011: 6).

The general or academic schooling track has two streams – the 'senior general secondary education' (HAVO) track which feeds into professional higher education (HBO), and the 'pre-university education' (VWO) track which links with 'university education' (WO). The basic structure of the system is illustrated in Figure 3:

FIGURE 3 The structure of the education system in the Netherlands

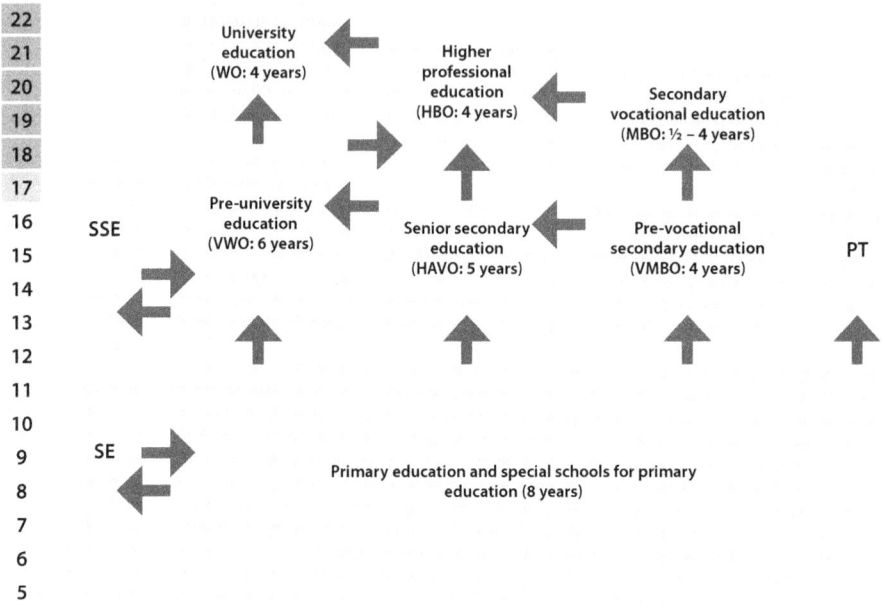

Source: Altinyelken, Du Bois-Reymond and Karsten (2010: 6).

Senior secondary vocational education (MBO)

Students in the MBO track choose to study in one of four broadly defined fields: technical; economic and administrative; services, health care and agriculture (Reubzaet *et al*, 2011: 6). Learning in the MBO track is both classroom- and work-based, and students choose between the two modes of provision:

1. **The work-based route (apprenticeship):** In 2010 this work-based pathway enrolled 34% of the MBO students (Visser, 2010: 15). A key feature of this route is that the work-based apprentices have an employment contract with an accredited employer, and they are paid the minimum wage. They typically spend 80% of their time as trainees in the workplace and 20% in college-based training. Students in this work-based route are found mostly in the technical sectors (metal, electronics, installation, building industry, and car mechanics), but numbers are also growing in the care and health sector, resulting in more and more women taking part in apprenticeships (Onstenk & Blokhuis, 2006: 35).
2. **The college-based route:** In 2010 this college-based pathway enrolled 66% of the MBO students (Visser, 2010: 15). It comprises students enrolled at one of the following training institutions: ROCs, specialist trade colleges, or agricultural training centres. The training may include one day a week at a workplace. Only accredited employers can provide training places to these students. The mix between classroom and workplace typically involves a minimum of 20% and a maximum of

60% of time spent in the workplace, during which the trainee receives on-the-job training and a small training allowance, but not a wage (Sung, 2010: 23-24).

Guaranteeing all students in the MBO level a work placement is a central feature of the Dutch system and requires the commitment of a large number of employers to induct and train young people. While companies are not legally obliged to take on TVET students, fiscal incentives are provided. For instance, for every student-employee, an employer can receive an incentive of €2 500 annually (Bewick & Abbott, 2010: 78).

The TVET component of post-school education and training has become a very large system. For example, vocational education consists of 35% of the secondary schooling system, and higher professional education – applied or polytechnic higher education – comprises 62% of all post-school tertiary training (Altinyelken, Du Bois-Reymond & Karsten, 2010: 24).

Employer buy-in

Sung, Raddon and Ashton (2006), who participated in a joint project reviewing nine different post-school systems in 2006, argue strongly that employer control of the Dutch system is critical to its success. Employers occupy a 'pivotal position' which enables them to 'lead' the skills development system through the sector skills councils – in this instance, the Knowledge Centres (Sung, Raddon & Ashton, 2009: 61-62). Employers are essentially the 'starting point' of an institutional virtuous circle. Through their Knowledge Centres, employers are able to identify the skills needs of each sector. Detailed job profiles of these skills needs are then fed to the Netherlands Association of VET Colleges (the BVE Raad), the umbrella body representing all the ROCs in the Netherlands. The ROCs then develop curricula based on these employer-defined occupational requirements (Raddon and Sung, 2006: 13). Once the curriculum is approved by government, the ROCs and employers both implement the training required – in the classroom at the ROCs and in the workplace (by employers). Employers are the primary training provider within the work-based pathway, which entails up to 80% of on-the-job training and 20% release for school-based training (Raddon & Sung, 2006: 13). Employers also have to offer work placements to learners from the school-based route. There are nearly 900 Knowledge Centre officials whose work it is to ensure that employers are accredited to perform this training role within the firm (Bewick and Abbott, 2010: 78). There are over 200 000 firms accredited to provide this training. All in all, it can be said that there is a high level of 'system alignment' between all these different institutional players and locales, creating a 'virtuous circle' of training and development (Sung, 2010: 21, 28-29).

Assessing the Dutch system

A number of strengths of the Dutch post-school system have been raised in the preceding discussion. Firstly, the Dutch TVET system benefits from the wider social solidarity underpinning Dutch economic and social life. Each social partner has a shared responsibility and collaborative role in each of the stages of the skills development system (Sung, 2010: 20). The actual content and the volume of training as well as who benefits is decided annually through collective bargaining agreements between employers and unions across all sectors of the Dutch economy (Sung *et al*, 2006: 64).

Secondly, the effective 'alignment' of the differing institutional components with each other provides strong complementarities across the entire TVET system. This is perhaps the most striking of the successful features of the Dutch system. The 'complementary' rather than 'contradictory' effects this alignment has across the system is why the Dutch system continues to work so well as a virtuous circle:

> *SSCs cannot function effectively if their operations are constrained or contradicted by other components of the VET system. The other components referred to here are crucially the flow of funding, the delivery of skills through the vocational education system, the determination of vocational qualifications, financial incentives for training, the support of unions and/or employees and the objectives of other relevant government agencies ... The cumulative reinforcement of all these various components produces a system that is highly sensitive to the skill needs of employers but, because of the involvement of the unions, is cognisant of the public interest. This is what we mean when we speak of the component parts of the system being aligned to the same objectives and being driven by the employers. (Ashton, 2006: 6–7)*

This is a very stable TVET system. Nijhof and Van Esch (2004) argue that the reforms of 1996 were bold and systemic. The Act was 'a clear and explicit attempt to plan the reforms systemically and to try to design a new system as a whole, rather than engage in a sequence of changes to isolated elements of the system, as has been the case in the UK over the past decades' (Nijhof & Van Esch, 2004: 258). The bold risks taken by the Dutch government in 1996 have paid off with two decades of growth and stability across a very integrated and aligned TVET system (Onstenk & Blokhuis, 2006: 33).

Conclusions

The differences in managing educational change could not be starker than those reflected by the UK and Netherlands case studies of TVET reform over the past three decades. The most important of these differences are captured in Table 5. They are represented as the archetypal differences between the two ideal-type systems of TVET – identified at the beginning of this chapter as the Central and Northern European 'social solidarity system' versus the more Anglo-Saxon inspired statist and prescriptive system of market driven TVET provision.

Table 5 suggests highly divergent outcomes in the global system of TVET after three decades of neo-liberal reform. On the one side are countries with very developed systems of cross-departmental coordination and social cooperation with other societal stakeholders which have acted to contain the destructive potential of neo-liberal reforms whilst retaining stability across the FE system. These countries have used the reforms to achieve greater system alignment and harmonisation.

On the other side, there are systems of TVET characterised by poor coordination and cooperation capabilities and with few linkages to societal stakeholders such as employers and unions. These systems have had no social safety net to cushion the destructive force

TABLE 5 Axes of differentiation in TVET systems globally

Axis of differentiation	Social solidarity TVET system, for example, as in the Netherlands	Statist, prescriptive systems of market-driven TVET, for example, as in the UK
1. Alignment	• Differing sub-components of the TVET system play a 'complementary' role towards each other	• System characterised by contradictory and unintended outcomes
2. Employer-led	• Employers have a major say in running the TVET system • TVET graduate outcomes are aligned to demand-side requirements	• There is an obsession with supply-side improvements as the basis for increasing competitiveness – which actually constitutes a misdiagnosis of the UK's competitiveness problems • Not all national vocational qualifications (NVQs) are recognised by employers: TVET graduates struggle to get jobs
3. Reform is comprehensive	• TVET change is comprehensive and its influence extends across multiple sub-systems, including the spheres of industrial policy and labour market requirements	• Change in TVET is not complemented by changes in economic, industrial, and labour market policies
4. Change is stable	• Change is stable with continuity across three decades of reforms • Individual changes are given time to evolve and consolidate before additional elements are added	• Change in TVET is discontinuous and highly disruptive, with each new five-year political administration leaving its own incoherent stamp on the system, often with dramatic reversals in the direction of reform
5. High-skill labour force	• A large proportion of the labour force gains access to post-school education and training because of these reforms	• Education remains exclusionary, with high drop-out rates at senior secondary school level and in the post-school system

of neo-liberal change and, as a consequence, have suffered immense institutional strain. Change has been discontinuous and unstable, with conditions worsening in many areas, including that of curriculum quality and TVET lecturer professionalism. System change has occurred mainly through imposition, forced compliance, and with considerable levels of resistance, mostly informal and hidden.

South Africa's path through TVET reform?

These two ideal-type global systems and the five axes of differentiation between the two systems provide a very useful template with which to analyse TVET reforms occurring in other countries in the world, including South Africa. As the other chapters in this book will show, the South African post-school and FE college system underwent immense institutional strain during the two decades of unrelenting reform since the advent of democracy in 1994, which included the insertion of new state performance measures, institutional mergers, and new curricula demands. All these changes, as in the UK trajectory described above, have created immense institutional instability. This occurred differently in South Africa in one important respect though – a high degree of institutional failure to pull the reforms successfully through, caused primarily by weak state capabilities to manage change. Successful change has also been weakened – as in the UK case – by various levels of forced compliance, institutional 'forgetfulness', and other forms of covert resistance.

Specific features of this change process in South Africa will be examined in the next chapters – including the reform of teaching and learning methodologies, as well as changes to institutional governance, performance management, and institutional evaluation. Evidence of the difficulties of change will be highlighted through reflections on a college change process initiated by JET Education Services (JET), the publishers of this book. This book seeks to highlight the lessons which can be learnt from the various change management initiatives, in order that these lessons inform future practice.

References

Altinyelken, H.K., Du Bois-Reymond, M., & Karsten, S. (2010). *Governance of educational trajectories in Europe: Country report, the Netherlands*. GOETE working paper. Amsterdam: University of Amsterdam.

Ashton, A. (2006). *Lessons from abroad: developing sector based approaches to skills*. SSDA Catalyst Issue 2. Wath-upon-Dearne: Sector Skills Development Agency.

Ashton, D. & Green, F. (1996). *Education, training and the global economy*. Cheltenham: Edward Elgar.

Ball, S. (2003). The teacher's soul and the terrors of performativity. *Journal of Education Policy*, 18(2): 215–28.

Ball, S.J. (2012). Performativity, commodification and commitment: An I-spy guide to the neo-liberal university. *British Journal of Educational Studies*, 60(1): 17–28.

Bewick, T. & Abbott, P., (Eds). (2010). *Think global, act sectoral*. London: International Network of Sector Skills Organisations (INSSO).

Boocock, A. (2013). Further education performance indicators: a motivational or a performative tool? *Research in Post-Compulsory Education*, 18(3): 309–325.

Brown, P., Green, A., & Lauder, H. (2001). *High skills, globalisation, competitiveness and skill formation*. Oxford: Oxford University Press.

Castells, M. (1996). *The rise of the network society: The information age*. Economy, society, and culture (Vol. 1). Oxford: Blackwell.

Cuddy, N. & Leney, T. (2005). *Vocational education and training in the United Kingdom: short description*. CEDEFOP (European Centre for the Development of Vocational Training). Panorama series, 111. Luxembourg, Office of Official Publications of the European Communities.

Fisher, R. & Simmons, R. (2012). Liberal conservatism, vocationalism and further education in England. *Globalisation, Societies and Education*, 10(1): 31–51.

Geurts, J. & Meijers, F. (2009). Vocational education in the Netherlands: In search of a new identity. Unpublished paper, Hague Technical University, The Hague, Netherlands.

Green, A., Mostafa, T., & Preston, J. (2010). *The chimera of competitiveness: varieties of capitalism and the economic crisis*. Centre for Learning and Life Chances in Knowledge Economies and

Societies (LLAKES). London: Institute of Education, University of London.

Hall, P.A. & Soskice, D., (Eds). (2001). *Varieties of capitalism: The institutional foundations of comparative advantage.* Oxford: Oxford University Press.

Hall, P.A. & Thelen, K. (2007). *Institutional change in varieties of capitalism.* Cambridge: Harvard University Press.

Harvey, D. (2005). *A brief history of neo-liberalism.* Oxford: Oxford University Press.

Keep, E. & James, S. (2012). A Bermuda triangle of policy? 'Bad jobs', skills policy and incentives to learn at the bottom end of the labour market. *Journal of Education Policy*, 27(2): 211–230.

Lanning, T. & Lawton, K. (2012). *No train no gain: Beyond free-market and state-led skills policy.* London: Institute for Public Policy Research.

Leathwood, C. & Read, B. (2013). Research policy and academic performativity: compliance, contestation and complicity. *Studies in Higher Education*, 38(8): 1162–1174.

Mather, K., Worrall, L., & Mather, G. (2012). Engineering compliance and worker resistance in UK further education: The creation of the Stepford lecturer. *Employee Relations*, 34(5): 534–554.

Nijhof, W.J. & Van Esch, W., (Eds). (2004). *Unravelling policy, power, process and performance: The formative evaluation of the Dutch Adult and Vocational Education Act.* Hertogenbosch: Centre for Innovation of Education and Training (CINOP).

O'Flynn, J. (2007). From new public management to public value: Paradigmatic change and managerial implications. *Australian Journal of Public Administration*, 66(3): 353–366.

Onstenk, J. & Blokhuis, F. (2006). Rediscovering apprenticeship in the Netherlands? Workshop paper number 13. In: Rauner, F. & Herrmann, I., (Eds). *Rediscovering apprenticeship: An answer to learning enterprises.* Germany: W. Bertelsmann Verlag.

Page, D. (2011). From principled dissent to cognitive escape: managerial resistance in the English further education sector. *Journal of Vocational Education & Training*, 63(1): 1–13.

Payne, J. (2007). *Sector skills councils and employer engagement – delivering the employer-led skills agenda in England.* Research paper number 78. Oxford: Research Centre on Skills, Knowledge and Organisational Performance (SKOPE), Cardiff and Oxford Universities.

Payne, J. & Keep, E. (2011). *One step forward, two steps back ? Skills policy in England under the Coalition Government.* Research paper number 102. Oxford: Research Centre on Skills, Knowledge and Organisational Performance (SKOPE), Cardiff and Oxford Universities.

Raddon, B.A. & Sung, J. (2006). *The role of employers in sectoral skills development: International approaches.* Working paper number 49. Leicester: Centre for Labour Market Studies, University of Leicester.

Republic of South Africa (RSA). (1998). *Education White Paper 4: A programme for the transformation of further education and training: Preparing for the twenty-first century through education, training and work.* Pretoria: Government Printer.

Reubzaet, I., Romme, I., & Geerstma, A. (2011). *Practical matters: what young people think about vocational education in the Netherlands.* London: City & Guilds Centre for Skills Development, United Kingdom.

Steedman, H. (2011). *Apprenticeship policy in England: Increasing skills versus boosting young people's job prospects.* London: Centre for Economic Performance (CPE), London School of Economics.

Steer, R., Spours, K., Hodgson, A., Finlay, I., Coffield, F., Edward, S., & Gregson, M. (2007). Modernisation and the role of policy levers in the learning and skills sector. *Journal of Vocational Education & Training*, 59(2): 175–192.

Sung, J. (2010). Vocational education and training and employer engagement: an industry-led sectoral system in the Netherlands. *International Journal of Training and Development*, 14(1): 16–31.

Sung, J., Raddon, A., & Ashton, D. (2006). *Skills abroad: A comparative assessment of international policy approaches to skills leading to the development of policy: Recommendations for the UK*. Research Report done for Skills for Business, Centre for Labour Market Studies, University of Leicester. United Kingdom: Sector Skills Development Agency.

UK Commission for Employment and Skills (UKCES). (2010). *What's the deal? The employer voice in the employment and skills system*. London: UK Commission for Employment and Skills.

Visser, K. (2010). *The Netherlands – VET in Europe: Country report*. ECBO Refernet and Cedefop. Thessaloniki, Greece: CEDEFOP.

Wolf, A. (2011). *Review of vocational education: The Wolf report*. London: Department of Further Education, Skills and Lifelong Learning.

chapter 2

UNFINISHED BUSINESS
MANAGING THE TRANSFORMATION OF FURTHER EDUCATION AND TRAINING COLLEGES

Anthony Gewer
TVET Consultant

Introduction

The South African government, as with most countries globally, has placed significant emphasis on the importance of technical and vocational education and training (TVET) for equipping young people to engage with an increasingly competitive and unpredictable labour market. This emphasis has emerged since 1998, around the same time as interest in TVET worldwide re-emerged, and was established off the back of a brief but intensive period of policy and legislative development which framed the evolution of TVET for the next decade. Core to this thinking was the creation of a sound pre-employment vocational education system that could complement the secondary schooling system and provide vocational pathways. To achieve this, the government sought to revitalise the technical colleges, whose role had disintegrated since the decline of the apprenticeship system towards the end of the last century.

From 2000 onwards, government embarked on a systemic restructuring of the technical colleges. This restructuring took the form of mergers, recapitalisation, recurriculation, expansion and, more recently, migration from the authority of provincial departments of education to that of the national Department of Higher Education and Training (DHET). The various phases of transformation since then have illustrated the significant challenges associated with trying to reinvent a system to meet the burgeoning demands of a democratic society. For much of the period 1998 to 2006, the college system operated without a strong identity, caught between the battles to remedy the schooling system and the emerging skills development institutions. The performance of the technical colleges (renamed further education and training or FET colleges following the mergers) received little focus during this period, with the emphasis being on restructuring and recapitalisation, rather than addressing fundamental issues about the identity of the colleges, the curriculum they offer, or the role they are expected to play.

Post-2006, there was a greater attempt to distinguish the FET colleges from the rest of the education and training system, and this distinction became more obvious when the colleges became part of an expanded post-school system in 2009, formally splitting from the schooling system. While the post-2009 period has seen significant quantitative growth in the college system, the performance and role of colleges has remained static since then.

Invariably, the transformation of the FET college system since 1998 has been shaped by the shifting ideological and political imperatives of government. While the sector initially followed a trend towards increased autonomy and market-led delivery, it was clear that such an approach would inevitably conflict with the government's agenda of redress, access, and equity. As a result, government, at various points, sought to direct and drive transformation centrally in the absence of a longer-term strategy, and this created mixed messages as to the policy trajectory for colleges. The manifestation of this is a system which has not yet realised full transformation, and still faces uncertainty and confusion as to its role in addressing the skills requirements for sustainable economic growth.

The foundations of TVET policy, 1994–1998

The foundation for a state-driven transformation agenda for vocational education and training was laid early on in the National Training Strategy Initiative (NTSI) (National

Training Board, 1994), which provided for a shift away from the market-led system that had been introduced by the apartheid government in the 1980s and a move towards a more structured, employer-led, competency-based system. The 'privatisation' of artisan training under the auspices of newly created Industry Training Boards resulted in the ultimate erosion of the apprenticeship system, with little uptake under the new system from the employers. As a result, there was a significant reduction in apprenticeship opportunities for youth that had benefited from the state-run system which had guaranteed access to on-the-job training, albeit in an unstructured and poorly monitored environment (Kraak, 2004).

This decline in apprenticeships and on-the-job training had particularly dire consequences for the technical college sector, which had traditionally provided the institutional training for the apprenticeships. The close working relationships between colleges and parastatals dissipated, and colleges became increasingly reliant on fee-paying students who were upgrading their qualifications with the hope of becoming employed, but who were not guaranteed access to workplace learning opportunities (Chisholm, 1992). For black students in township colleges, programmes were limited to low-level technical and commercial subjects, and there was minimal access to artisan training.

Despite the increasing number of black youth participating in technical training from the 1980s onwards, these students were restricted to state colleges which were poorly resourced and highly regulated under the strict control of the former Department of Education and Training (DET). White students continued to benefit from better resourced and more autonomous state-aided colleges.

While the need for institutional reform of technical colleges was a glaring challenge for the new democratic government, the broader configuring of the education and training system following the NTSI laid the basis for the further degradation of the college system. Technical colleges were excluded from the emerging post-apartheid skills development regime of the Department of Labour, continuing to operate within the Ministry of Education. Given the division between education outside of the workplace under the Ministry of Education and occupational training for the workplace under the Department of Labour, it was inevitable that the colleges would increasingly become limited in their ability to directly engage with and respond to industry.

The Education White Paper 4: A Programme for the Transformation of Further Education and Training (RSA, 1998a), which laid the foundation for the Further Education and Training Act No. 98 of 1998 (RSA, 1998b), grappled with how to create a clear identity for colleges within the FET band of the National Qualifications Framework (NQF) alongside secondary schools, rather than with the broader role of the colleges in addressing the skills needs of the economy. The White Paper viewed the FET band as an integrated system with a strong interface between secondary schools and colleges, overcoming the traditional distinctions between academic and vocational education, but simultaneously recognising that bringing these two institutional forms together would present a number of legislative and policy challenges.

The FET White Paper also highlighted the need for an institutional context that would allow increased autonomy and flexibility in the delivery of vocational programmes, requiring a new funding framework and a new institutional form. The subsequent FET

Act provided provincial education ministers with the power to create these newly formed institutions through a process of mergers which would bring state and state-aided colleges together and overcome past distinctions and resource inequality. This process of integration would be phased in on the basis of clear institutional plans, and these colleges would need to demonstrate their ability to manage their funds appropriately. The intention was to pilot the new institutional framework by fast tracking a few stronger institutions and testing out the delegated budgetary authority that would be required under the new funding regime.

The first stage of implementation: Mergers and restructuring

Over the decade following 1991, the college sector grew from a base of 39 000 full-time equivalent (FTE) students (Chisholm, 1992) to around 139 000 in 2000 (Powell & Hall, 2002). During this period, there was a significant shift in the student profile – white students made up 67% of the student population in 1991 (Chisholm, 1992), and by 2000 this had shifted to 75% African and only 12% white (Powell & Hall, 2002). The historical distinctions between state and state-aided colleges remained intact, and furthermore, during this period, the racial make-up of staff and the racial profile of governing councils did not change much. White teaching and management staff predominated, particularly in state-aided colleges, and the racial profile of councils continued to be divided on similar lines.

Following the promulgation of the FET Act, it was expected that provincial departments of education would drive the implementation of institutional restructuring to address these imbalance and inequities. However, by 2000, very little progress had been made on the implementation of the FET Act. The Gauteng, KwaZulu-Natal, and Western Cape provinces had initiated research into the state of colleges,[3] and the Western Cape Department of Education developed a Master Plan which incorporated an institutional re-organisation plan, but this had not yet been implemented.

In 1999, following the initial studies in Gauteng and the Western Cape and based on the findings thereof, the National Business Initiative (NBI) initiated a five-year private sector funded programme, the Colleges Collaboration Fund (CCF), to support the restructuring and development of the colleges. The CCF model drew heavily on the market-driven systems of the United Kingdom (UK) and Australia, seeking to incentivise change in the college system through financial and technical assistance. Drawing on the policy and legislative frameworks, the programme sought to support provincial departments of education to fast track the implementation of the FET Act based on the stipulations in the FET White Paper, and further develop the governance and management capacity of the colleges to ensure that the restructuring process would have an effective and sustainable outcome.

The NBI extended the situational analyses that had been done in Gauteng, the Western Cape and KwaZulu-Natal to all nine provinces to provide the basis for the restructuring plan in each province. In addition, through a government-to-government agreement

---

3   Fisher, Hall and Jaff (1998); Kraak and Hall (1999) and National Business Initiative (1999) respectively.

between South Africa and the UK, the NBI initiated the Tirisano Fellowship, an international exchange programme aimed at placing (particularly black) middle managers for a three-month period in a UK college to develop their skills in a specialised area of college management under the mentorship of a UK college mentor. The fellowship's key objective was to address equity issues in middle management by targeting black and female middle managers.

The situational analyses of the nine provinces provided insight into the severe weaknesses in the capacity of both the provincial departments of education and the colleges themselves. On the basis of these findings, and given the delays in meaningful progress in implementing the FET Act, the national Department of Education (DoE) in 2001 embarked on a nationally driven process of planning. Provincial departments were tasked with developing provincial restructuring plans, with the key focus on merging institutions based on size and proximity. The merger of institutions was expected to bring about increased efficiencies, responsiveness, and equity across colleges. A rapid process of merger facilitation was undertaken at each of the identified clusters of colleges. Merger plans were completed within a period of three months in each of the newly merged colleges, and new councils were established in 2002.

The relationships between provincial departments of education and the colleges under their control varied from province to province, but in general there was limited capacity or support available to colleges in many provinces. While there were dedicated FET directorates in each province, in most cases these were poorly resourced, and the officials therein were thinly stretched in trying to provide colleges with meaningful support. With the exception of the Western Cape, the provincial departments of education did not assign priority to the colleges. As a result, the DoE created the national framework for the merger process, which the provinces and colleges were expected to implement. This rapid change process proved difficult for both provincial officials and college officials, given the limited capacity and support available on the ground.

For colleges, the merger process involved bringing together institutions with vastly different organisational cultures, identities, and resource bases. In a case study of the merger of three colleges in Tshwane, Sooklal (2004) illustrates the extent to which the colleges were forced into the merger process without effective support. The flow of communication to staff around the merger was weak, and there were high levels of resistance, particularly from staff from the previously 'white' college. The tensions associated with race and cultural beliefs were not effectively addressed, and this hindered the integration of the three institutions. There was a lack of clarity around leadership and lines of accountability during the initial period of the merger, restricting decision-making and further adding to the instability in the colleges. Ultimately, the manner in which the merger was managed represented a missed opportunity for meaningful transformation, and the potential benefits of the merger in this regard were not realised.

This case study represents the common challenges that were being experienced in colleges across the country at the time. The absence of leadership at the institutional level during the merger period was a cause for anxiety and tension throughout the system. Principals of pre-merged colleges were not meaningfully brought into the process, and staff were unsure of to whom they should be accountable. The support provided to the colleges in the form of merger facilitators assisted in moving the merger processes forward rapidly, but led to variable outputs, and did not provide an optimal environment for stakeholder engagement. In some cases, it was the facilitators themselves, despite having little understanding of the college sector, who wrote the merger plans, with little input from stakeholders in the colleges.

While the new colleges were declared and councils were appointed soon after the merger plans were completed, the process of appointment of new principals was prolonged, and was only completed in all provinces by mid-2003 (Gewer, 2005). The colleges therefore operated in a situation of relative uncertainty during this time, as staff awaited the new leadership, and were uncertain about the impact of the restructuring process on positions in the colleges.

One of the key outcomes of the merger process was to consolidate enrolments in the college system, so as to enhance scale and efficiencies. Prior to the mergers, 70% of colleges enrolled fewer than 1 000 FTEs, and following the mergers, 78% of the newly merged colleges enrolled more than 1 000 FTEs (DoE, 2004c). In addition, the merger process did succeed in its intent to combine smaller and weaker colleges with stronger colleges so as to create a more equitable institutional base. An indication of this outcome is that in 1998, prior to the mergers, 26% of senior staff in colleges were black, and 74% were white. By 2002, 41% were black, and 59% were white. However, due to the manner in which the merger process was managed, the strengthening and repositioning of the colleges to respond to social and economic demands was not necessarily realised (DoE, 2004c).

The second phase of transformation: Institutional differentiation

Despite the intentions underlying the restructuring of the FET landscape, the 50 newly merged FET colleges still faced a number of historical obstacles to meaningful reform. Many of the issues facing colleges prior to the mergers remained. The limited scope of programmes offered, the bias towards theory, and the generally weak relationships between colleges and industry continued to plague colleges. The large investment by the private sector in the CCF had supported the broad restructuring of the sector, but had done little to bring about improvement in management, or in the quality of teaching and learning in the colleges.

The DoE had elected to focus the efforts of the CCF on the national restructuring plan. The CCF investment in management development was largely assigned to the Tirisano Fellowship programme, which was geared to developing a future corps of middle management that could drive transformation post-restructuring. The fellows were exposed to a range of best practices in UK colleges, with the expectation that they would be able to bring these practices back to the restructured colleges. Due to the high levels of instability in the college sector during and immediately following the mergers, the contribution of the fellows was largely restricted, and many were treated with a certain level of disdain. Nonetheless, the role of the Tirisano fellows became increasingly valuable during the merger planning (Gewer, 2005). In the aftermath of the mergers, opportunities were created for fellows to move into leadership roles in the colleges, or be integrally involved in the development and implementation of new policies, particularly in the areas of student support and quality assurance. The scope of the fellows' contribution was determined by the emerging leadership in the colleges, and despite fellows' initial frustrations over the lack of support on their return, the programme eventually changed the racial profile of management, and contributed to more effective policy development.

However, the extent to which new innovative practice could be brought into the colleges was still inhibited by their weak identity and limited scope of provision. While the FET Act had enabled the merger and renaming of colleges, their status within the FET band still remained on the periphery of the secondary schooling system. The college curriculum remained intact, and there was no framework for curriculum diversification or funding of new programmes. While there was an initial increase in 'non-DoE' programmes during the period 1998 to 2000, suggesting some shift away from the traditional programmes, this increase slowed in the period 2000–2002 (the merger period), and enrolment in these programmes represented only 14% of the total full-time enrolment in 2002 (DoE, 2004c).

Similarly, despite the intent in White Paper 4 to link colleges to the Sector Education and Training Authorities (SETAs), there had been little engagement by 2002. There was little involvement of colleges in learnership provision (DoE, 2004a), with the exception of those campuses that already had track records and resources in certain occupational fields, and were approached by companies or SETAs to participate in learnership initiatives. In addition, the large-scale roll-out of strategic National Skills Fund (NSF) projects through SETAs as part of the Department of Labour's National Skills Development Strategy represented an important opportunity for colleges to develop responsive occupational programmes linked to key sectors (e.g FIETA Shintsha Project, FoodBev Learnership Project, BANKSETA Learnership Project). However, it was clear that such learnership programmes would invariably only benefit a relatively small number of students, given the funding and systemic challenges faced.

In line with the DoE's strategy to support the 50 merged colleges and to raise their profiles, the period 2005–2008 represented a significant phase of policy implementation. The DoE sought to actively increase the levels of autonomy in the 50 merged colleges so as to create the space for them to realise a more distinct role alongside secondary schools. This involved four key activities: a recapitalisation programme, redefining the identity of the colleges, developing a new curriculum, and establishing a new funding regime.

Recapitalisation

The DoE requested a recapitalisation grant from the National Treasury to fund the upgrading and development of infrastructure and capacity in the colleges to implement programmes which would address the 11 priority skills areas (DoE Budget Vote, 2004/05).

The recapitalisation programme flowed from the Financial and Institutional Review conducted by the consulting firm KPMG through funding from the CCF (DoE, 2004b). As part of this exercise, KPMG analysed the level of investment needed to achieve equity across the newly merged colleges with respect to infrastructure. Based largely on an analysis of the merger plans, KPMG calculated that an injection of R1.8 billion was needed to 'level the playing field' and 'sustain operations at the Colleges' (DoE, 2004b). In its report, KPMG highlighted the importance of treating the register of needs generated as part of the merger process with some caution, given that the register was viewed as a wish list in some cases, rather than a practical analysis of the college's needs. However, the analysis provided an estimate of the aggregate investment needed to develop the merged colleges. In 2003, KPMG also developed a financial management toolkit, and 10 colleges were identified as high risk and provided with short-term, intensive financial management support.

Between 2004 and 2005, the National Treasury approved a R1.9 billion recapitalisation grant for all 50 colleges, most of which was earmarked for development or upgrading of infrastructure, purchasing of equipment, and training of staff. The total allocation was divided over four years, a preparatory year followed by three years of actual implementation. In 2005/06, R50 million was allocated to the DoE for planning and preparation of the college sector procurement and finance systems. The DoE commissioned a range of research to establish the baseline and set targets for the recapitalisation programmes. Colleges were required to develop recapitalisation plans in seven strategic management areas, namely human resource development (HRD), systems and procedures, refurbishment of infrastructure, building or purchasing new infrastructure, refurbishing of campus sites, equipment, and curriculum support.

While plans initially had a strong focus on the delivery of learnerships and skills programmes, this focus was revised and placed on introduction of the new National Certificate Vocational (NCV) programmes. The DoE was clearly preparing colleges for the introduction of the curriculum, with a view that the NCV would form the basis for future growth and development in college programme delivery. A portion of the grant was earmarked for the upgrading of 2 000 lecturers to deliver the NCV programmes, and this was complemented by training for a further 6 000 lecturers by the DoE over the three-year period. Generally, the recapitalisation programme was well managed across the provinces, and the colleges met their expenditure against plan, with close monitoring from the DoE and the provincial departments of education. However, the primary focus on the NCV further suggested that engagement of the colleges in learnerships and occupationally driven training was unlikely to materialise.

Redefining colleges

The second key measure to support the evolution of the 50 merged colleges was to create more clarity in law as to the distinct identity of the colleges vis-à-vis the secondary schooling system which operated alongside them in the further education and training band. Under the Further Education and Training Colleges Act No. 16 of 2006, (RSA, 2006), colleges would be renamed as 'FET Colleges' rather than 'FET Institutions'. This meant that while FET colleges would still operate primarily in the further education and training band of the education system, they could be assigned more autonomy and be given distinct powers.

In order to further reinforce this new identity, and to enable colleges to respond more effectively to the demand for skills, the FET Act of 2006 provided for college educators and administrative staff to come under the employ of the colleges, rather than the state. This would allow colleges to organise their staff in a manner that would allow for more responsive delivery and was based on the assumption that the colleges required such autonomy in order to effectively deliver on the emerging NCV curriculum in the context of market competition and the demand for quality vocational education. In essence, the Act sought to position colleges as institutions of choice.

The promulgation of this Act implied a blanket move towards institutional autonomy, which was an important shift from the rhetoric in the FET White Paper which had suggested a more developmental approach towards autonomy, based on the capacity and resources of the colleges. While the recapitalisation programme had ostensibly contributed to levelling the playing field in terms of infrastructure, the management and governance capacity in colleges was still highly variable, and while colleges had benefited from the Tirisano Fellowship and other donor-funded management development initiatives, the post-merger college structures still lacked sufficient management experience, particularly in the management of large multi-campus institutions. The FET Colleges Act would require colleges to take on responsibility for the employment of large numbers of teaching and administrative staff, in addition to implementing a vastly different curriculum and a new funding regime. In terms of the Act, all public FET colleges were deemed to be autonomous, regardless of their management and governance capacity.

The effect of the Act was to create high levels of anxiety amongst college staff, as they faced the decision of whether to move into the employ of the colleges, which would threaten the security of their employment, or remain employed by the provincial departments of education (the latter would mean that they could be redeployed away from the college to another position within the provincial education departments). As a result of this instability, there was an exodus from the colleges of some staff who chose to either remain with the provinces or move out of the education system.

While the scope of this exodus is not clear, there was general concern over the capacity of the governing councils to act as employers and there was confusion over the role of the provincial departments of education who still held the purse strings (continuing to administer the payroll of the conditional grant allocation) and could determine the appointment of staff. In addition, the principals of the colleges continued to be accountable to the provincial education departments rather than to the councils, which limited the role of the councils in driving performance improvement. The situation also created internal tensions between staff who were still on the state payroll and still enjoying state benefits, and those staff who were employed on college contracts, and therefore did not enjoy the same job security and benefits.

This instability was acknowledged in 2011[4] after the newly formed Department of Higher Education and Training (DHET) had started the process to take control of the FET colleges, and the DHET sought to regularise the employment of all college staff to bring college employees onto an even footing and further transfer them back to the employ of the state. In the intervening years since promulgation of the FET Colleges Act of 2006, the employment conditions of staff in colleges had been a source of constant tension.

While the intention of the Act was to increase the autonomy of the colleges, the implementation of the Act further exposed the weak capacity of colleges to govern themselves. There was limited capacity in the provincial departments of education to support the colleges in this transition, and the decision by the DoE to force colleges to

---

4   Address by the Minister of Higher Education and Training, during parliamentary debate on the Further Education and Training Colleges, Cape Town (20/09/2011).

adopt a new identity while still seeking to create stability and cohesion in the aftermath of the mergers only created further mistrust and disillusionment amongst staff. This state of affairs raised the question of the readiness of colleges to operate autonomously and engage in market competition, given the range of unresolved internal issues and the relative immaturity of the system post-merger. In particular, the readiness of governing councils to take on the responsibility of employing large numbers of staff, given the variability in their levels of expertise and experience, was in question.

In effect, a rigorous analysis of the state of readiness of the colleges should have been done as stipulated in the FET White Paper, and a stronger focus on development should have been undertaken to avoid the instability and negative impact on management and staff. The college context that was inherited by the DHET after 2009 highlighted these problems. The approach of providing gradual autonomy to those colleges that had the capacity to govern themselves could perhaps have provided the basis for developing an appropriate model and formula for self-governance.

Curriculum transformation
The third key element of driving the colleges forward post-merger was the introduction of a new curriculum that would be relevant to the needs of the economy. The intention behind the NCV was to more strategically position colleges to address priority skills demands by delivering sound general-vocational programmes that would prepare young people for entry into the workplace. The NCV should also provide a viable alternative pathway for young people who had completed Grade 9 and wished to follow a vocational pathway. The NCV should assist colleges to overcome the legacy of the N-programmes which had limited the scope of college provision and inhibited the employability of college students. The NCV would provide the equivalent of a vocational matric at Level 4 of the NQF.

The recapitalisation had been explicitly geared to preparing colleges to introduce the NCV, from both an infrastructural and capacity perspective. However, the delivery of the NCV presented a number of institutional challenges. The new curriculum required a shift away from trimester and semester programmes to a three-year qualification, which significantly altered timetabling and required the colleges to deliver the curriculum to fewer students for longer periods of time. In addition, while the N-programmes were being phased out, colleges were required to run the NCV and N-programmes simultaneously. In many cases, colleges would use the same lecturers to deliver both programmes, resulting in lecturers having little time for preparation and marking. Colleges also had to bring in a stronger focus on the foundational skills (English, Mathematics and Life Skills), as well as integrate theory and practice in the vocational subjects (through workshop practice). These requirements were particular challenges for colleges that did not have the teaching personnel to cope with the demands of the language and Mathematics curricula and had not provided practical workshop training in the past.

In a study of Engineering, Construction, and IT lecturers in 2009, the NBI found that two thirds of these lecturers had no teaching qualifications, a third had no technical qualifications, and only 41% had technical qualifications above Level 5 on the NQF (NBI, 2010). Similarly, the HSRC found that 57% of college lecturing staff nationally have less than a degree/higher diploma (Cosser, Kraak & Winnaar, 2011). A national study of lecturers across a range of fields in 2011 found that half the lecturers had no industry experience, and the majority had been in the college for fewer than five years (NBI, 2011). The increased demands of the curriculum placed significant pressure on these lecturers, and there had been limited time to address the capacity gaps. Despite the high level of investment in training of lecturers prior to the introduction of the NCV through the recapitalisation programme, these studies pointed to a substantial deficiency in the teaching capacity of college lecturers, and a more comprehensive programme to upgrade their skills and qualifications was required.

The second challenge related to the target group. The NCV assumed that the schooling system would have equipped young Grade 9s to exit the system and cope with the cognitive demands of the curriculum. With the first group of enrolments in 2007, colleges were not discerning in their selection, and of the 26 541 students enrolled at Level 2 nationally, only 4 490 were still enrolled at Level 4 in 2009, and 1 194 met the requirements for certification at the end of 2009. Increasingly, colleges became more selective about their entry criteria, and by 2009, 53% of college students were found to have achieved a Grade 12 matriculation certificate (Gewer, 2010). Colleges indicated that these matriculants coped better with the demands of the NCV, and by 2011, the NCV examinations results were demonstrating signs of improvement. However, the drive to rapidly massify the enrolments in NCV courses inhibited the capacity of colleges to bring about improvements in performance. The National Plan for Further Education and Training Colleges in 2008 (DoE, 2008) set the target of 800 000 enrolments in the NCV by 2014 off the base of 25 000. This translated into between 43% and 46% growth per annum.

The poor performance of students in the NCV programmes represented a threat to achieving this growth, creating an obstacle to colleges taking on new enrolments and also a negative perception of the NCV. After the weak results of the first cohort of NCV students in 2007, the DoE introduced a concession for colleges to allow NCV students progression to the next level of the qualification having passed only four of the seven required subjects. This exacerbated the blockages, as students who were carrying subjects that they could not pass had to extend their time to qualification, or drop out.

In effect, the NCV did not realise this massive growth in student enrolments. While the DoE had provided bursaries for NCV students from 2007 through the National Student Financial Aid Scheme (NSFAS), the number of students who could benefit from this scheme was limited, and the fees required from students were substantially higher than those required for the trimester and semester programmes. In addition, the high cost of the programme, combined with the poor throughput rates, restricted the number of new students that colleges could enrol. By 2009, when the National Plan took effect, there were 122 921 NCV enrolments in colleges, which was in line with the National Plan. However, it was clear that the targets could not be reached through the NCV alone.

The third stage of transformation: Moving to a consolidated post-school system

Despite extensive efforts to redefine and distinguish the FET college system, there were clear signs in 2009 that colleges were struggling to implement the range of policies that emerged during the second period of transformation and had begun to stagnate and even regress. There were high levels of dysfunctionality in some provinces (notably Limpopo, the Eastern Cape, and KwaZulu-Natal), the throughput rates were not improving significantly, and there were persistent levels of tension within the colleges regarding employment conditions.

The splitting of the Department of Education and the resultant creation of a Department of Higher Education and Training laid the foundation for wrestling the colleges away from the provinces and bringing them into a national framework. Many of the persistent challenges were perceived to be symptomatic of poor management and support on the part of most provinces. The colleges also became part of the newly elected government's Plan of Action, through which a Delivery Agreement was signed between the President and the new Minister of Higher Education and Training. This delivery agreement outlined targets for increased enrolments and improved throughput in the FET colleges over a five-year period. Importantly, while the Delivery Agreement set targets for increased access to post-Grade 12 programmes (i.e. N4–N6), it did not provide targets for increased enrolments in NCV programmes. Rather, the Delivery Agreement focused on increased throughput of students in the NCV[5] programmes.

In order to give effect to the migration process, a protocol was signed between the Minister and Director-General of the DHET and their provincial counterparts, whereby they agreed to work collaboratively and take no decisions without consultation. This agreement would overcome conflicts of inter-government relations regarding FET colleges until the formal transfer took place, and enable the DHET to drive college transformation at a national level in line with the Minister's Delivery Agreement.

A key priority was the targets for increased enrolments. Given the low prospects for massive growth, the low throughput, and the general uncertainty and discomfort amongst industry with respect to the NCV, the newly formed DHET extended the phasing out of the N-programmes in 2010.[6] Those colleges that had begun to phase out the programmes were now required to reinstate them. In addition, the funding that had been allocated through a conditional grant to fund NCV students would now have to be split between students in NCV and N-programmes, further limiting growth in NCV enrolment numbers.

Thus began the DHET's programme to massively speed up the rate of growth in FET colleges. Between 2010 and 2013, the college student population grew from 420 000 to around 709 000 (DHET report to Parliament, February 2015). This growth was accompanied by an increase in the budget allocation from R3.3 billion in 2009 to R5.8 billion in 2014. Simultaneously, the bursary allocation for FET college students grew from R300 million in 2009 to R2.1 billion in 2014. Despite this increase in budget, the relative size of the FET college budget to the total education budget remained static

---

5   Department of Higher Education and Training, Delivery Agreement 5: A Skilled and capable workforce to support an inclusive growth path.

6   Originally the Department of Education intended to phase out N1–N3 programmes by the end of 2006 and N4–N6 programmes by December 2011. The Minister of Higher Education and Training then extended the phasing out of the N4–N6 programmes to December 2013 and the N1–N3 programmes until the Quality Council for Trade and Occupations (QCTO) had developed appropriate occupational qualifications.

(around 2.5%), and colleges were continuing to enrol more students without sufficient subsidies to cover the numbers being enrolled. A task team report[7] on Funding and Planning in FET Colleges ahead of the FET Summit in 2010 found that many colleges were enrolling in excess of their approved budget allocation, causing them to operate at a loss. It was estimated that bad debt in colleges was around R83.6 million in 2008/09, particularly due to non-payment from NCV students. The expectations of free tuition had emerged as a result of the introduction of the national bursary scheme, and it was proving difficult to dampen these expectations. As a result, many students were not paying for their courses, or dropping out because they did not have sufficient finance.

Despite this, colleges continued to grow, and in his 2014 budget speech to Parliament, the Minister of Higher Education expressed confidence that the target of 800 000 would be reached in 2014. The large portion of this growth has been achieved in the N-programmes. The N1–N3 Engineering programmes, which had traditionally served the apprenticeship systems, grew off a base of 8 000 in 2010 to 117 000 in 2013 (DHET enrolment data). While N1–N3 Engineering had been reintroduced to provide a supply of candidates into artisan training, these students would be unlikely to find workplaces where they could undertake apprenticeships.

FIGURE 4 FET College enrolments by programme 2011–2013 (calculated using DHET enrolment data)

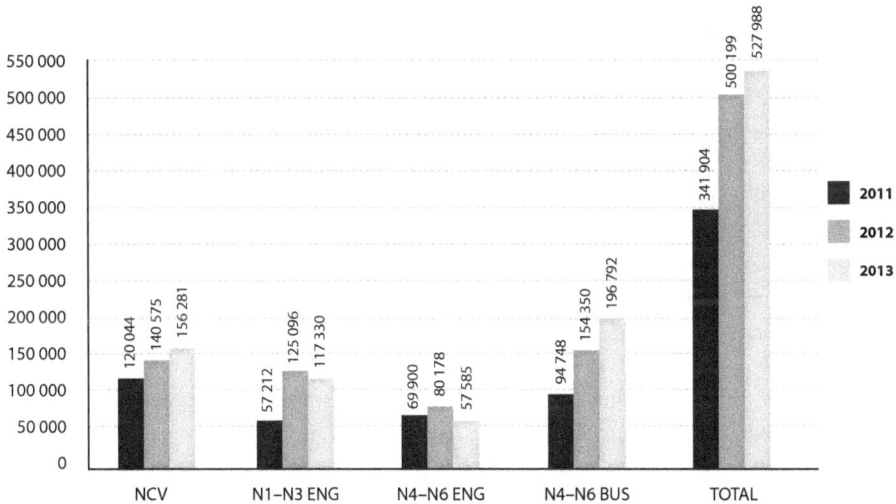

The N4–N6 programmes (for post-Grade 12s) experienced growth off a base of 71 000 in 2010 to 254 000 in 2013. A large part of this growth was in the Business Studies programmes, which offered limited prospects for employment.

By 2013, therefore, the headcount in N-programmes had jumped to 371 707 nationally, and colleges were placed under severe pressure to cope with these additional enrolments. Students flooded into the N-programmes because they were shorter in duration, cheaper,

---

7   Report to the FET Summit – Task Team 3: Planning and Funding for 2011 and Beyond. 23 August 2010.

and perceived to be easier than the NCV. However, the reintroduction of the N-programmes contributed to further instability in colleges. The increase in student numbers required the colleges to re-orientate their resource allocations, which had been set up to accommodate the full-scale implementation of the NCV. While the directive from the DHET was to manage the expansion according to available resources and capacity, many colleges enrolled beyond what their budgets and resources would allow, extending N-programmes into the afternoons and evenings, and engaging lecturing staff on a contract basis, or paying existing staff overtime to deliver these programmes. The dual delivery of NCV subjects and N-programmes during the day placed additional pressure on lecturers, impacting on preparation and marking time.

Some college staff welcomed the reintroduction of the N-programmes – they were better known and understood by both industry and the general public, and they were cheaper and less resource-intensive to run. However, despite the N-programmes being less onerous than the NCV for both the colleges and the students (they only required four subjects and no practical instruction), students' results in the N-programmes were similarly weak, with between 35 and 40% of students successfully completing (DHET Examinations data). Although the reintroduction of the N-programmes allowed for more rapid growth at a fraction of the cost of the NCV, it also resulted in confusion and the undoing of the extensive efforts on the part of colleges to promote and develop the NCV. There was an emerging sense that the NCV was a valuable programme that should prepare students well for entry into the workplace. However, the pressure on the DHET to grow the colleges and the relative cost of the NCV have had a negative effect on realising the NCV's potential and have rather allowed the colleges to regress into the comfort of the narrow N-programmes which offer limited scope for employability. This was illustrated in two tracer studies of Engineering graduates from N1–N3 programmes in 2001 and 2003 (Gewer, 2009). In these studies, Gewer found that only 25% of graduates were in employment, only 50% of whom were in a job related to their qualification. A key factor in ensuring employability was having access to work experience/workplace learning during studies. Across these two cohorts, 83% of these graduates received no work experience while studying, and 53% of those who did find work experience did so on their own, rather than through assistance from the colleges. No data exists on the employability of NCV graduates, although informal discussions with employers in the manufacturing and construction sector suggest that NCV graduates are of a higher calibre than those that have graduated with N-programmes.

The effect of the massive growth in student numbers has also been felt in the performance of students. In 2009, the NCV was producing an average pass rate of 9.55% at Level 2. By 2012, the average certification rate at Level 2 had increased to 42.6% (DHET Examinations data), indicating substantial improvement in performance during this period. However, while there had been a steady increase in performance between 2009 and 2011, there was a drop in Level 2 performance between 2011 and 2012, from 44.8% to 42.6%. In addition, the retention rates for NCV Level 2 students dropped from 61% to 48%. Similarly, the 2012 examination results for N4–N6 indicate an average 23% success rate, compared to 36% in 2011. This general decline in performance occurred in the context of a 64% increase in headcount enrolments from 400 273 in 2011 (DHET, 2013) to 657 690 in 2012 (DHET, 2014). With the anticipated increase to over 800 000 students in 2016 (double the 2011 enrolment), there is likely to be a further decline in student performance.

Ultimately, the migration of colleges from the provinces to the DHET has enabled significant growth in the sector after a decade of relative stagnation. The elevation of the sector to the post-school arena has created the impetus for growth, as government seeks to actively tackle the rising concern of youth unemployment and disengaged youth. However, the migration has also unveiled persistent challenges that continue to threaten stability in colleges and undermine their ability to fully realise their role in a national post-school system.

In the first instance, the DHET had to address the governance issues across the sector. With the migration to the DHET, the authority for appointment of governing councils shifted to the Minister of Higher Education and Training, in terms of the FET Colleges Amendment Act No. 3 of 2012. The DHET inherited councils that had variable functionality and legitimacy. At the time of this transfer of authority, finally in April 2013, the terms of the councils of 28 colleges across four provinces, including three which had the highest risk colleges (Limpopo, KwaZulu-Natal and Eastern Cape), had already expired. Other councils' terms lapsed before the Minister was able to reappoint new members. As a result, councils in these colleges were operating without legitimate authority, and there were concerns that many of their decisions could be found to be invalid if challenged. This placed the principal in a highly precarious and vulnerable position as the accounting officer, as it invariably indicated shortfalls in financial accountability and other forms of governance. The situation resulted in a protracted governance vacuum, and there were no guidelines to colleges on how to respond. Principals continued to operate without effective controls. Where councils had dedicated and committed members, the functions of the councils were able to continue largely unhindered, allowing a certain level of stability. In many cases, however, the active involvement of governing councils subsided or ceased until the Minister was finally able to appoint new councils in 2014, and the governance of the colleges was highly unstable.

The second challenge that the DHET has had to grapple with is the funding regime for colleges. Funding challenges exist at various levels of the system. In the first instance, the available budget allocation for colleges remains a key obstacle to growth. Despite the substantial growth in student numbers over the past five years, the budget for colleges still remains at around 2.4% of total education spend in the country, having been at this level since 2006. This has placed significant pressure on the system at all levels, given that the budget barely catered for the number of students who were enrolled in 2010. The DHET has increasingly sought additional complementary funding from the National Skills Fund and the SETAs, but funding still represents an ever-present obstacle.

Secondly, the flow of funding from National Treasury to colleges has been a persistent source of frustration since the DHET came into being. Despite the gradual migration of colleges to the DHET, the funding for colleges has continued to flow through the provincial administrations, negatively impacting the effective disbursement of funds to the FET colleges and their cash flow status. Colleges in some provinces continue to receive less funding than anticipated and do not receiving the funding according to the stipulated timeframes. As of 2014, the DHET has introduced amendments to the funding norms, which will remove the Provincial Education Departments from the planning and administration of funding for FET colleges. However, while the DHET took formal responsibility for colleges as of 1 April 2013, the transfer of the funding mechanism has still not taken effect, and provinces continue to be the conduit for the flow of funding.

At an institutional level, colleges display variable effectiveness in their financial management systems. The weak financial management capacity in many colleges was acknowledged by the Minister of Higher Education and Training in 2012, and a programme to install temporary chief financial officers (CFOs) through the South African Institute of Chartered Accountants was put in place in that year. The mandate of these acting CFOs was to stabilise and enhance the financial management systems in colleges, as well as to transfer skills to ensure these systems can be maintained.

In the Eastern Cape, an assessment of the financial management systems at the end of 2011 by JET found the systems to be primitive, with outdated recordkeeping, weak financial policies, and limited financial management skills. College budgets were controlled at central office, and campuses had little influence on the allocation of budgets or the procurement of materials. As such, colleges were unable to effectively track programme expenditure. At a macro level, this has made it impossible to accurately measure whether or not the funding received by colleges actually covers the real cost of programme delivery.[8] It also implies that the annual operational plans prepared by colleges are unlikely to accurately reflect actual budget requirements and will invariably result in a funding gap. The appointment of the acting CFOs has hopefully brought some stability to the financial management systems, but it is likely that many colleges will not have resolved the persistent shortcomings in financial management.

The third critical challenge that the DHET has faced is resolving the employment conditions in colleges. As indicated above, the 2006 Act had created a high level of anxiety and instability amongst staff, and the implementation of the Act had contributed to complexities in the conditions of employment of teaching staff in particular. In the first instance, there were persistent discrepancies between teaching staff previously employed by the state and now employed on a permanent basis by the college councils, and those teaching staff employed on contract by the colleges. The former enjoyed state benefits and job security, while the latter were subject to contract renewals and did not enjoy many benefits, placing them in a highly insecure and vulnerable position. This was a recipe for persistent internal tensions.

The Act had also disadvantaged those lecturers who moved from state to council employ. As a result of their shift to council employ, teaching staff who were former state employees did not enjoy the occupation-specific dispensation afforded to teachers in schools.[9]

The DHET has sought to reverse the effects of the Act, while simultaneously addressing inequities in the employment conditions of staff. In August 2010, an agreement was

---

8   Colleges are funded according to a funding formula which translates into unit cost per student, depending on the number of teaching posts.

9   The OSD was a customised remuneration dispensation for educators which extended the salary bands and thereby provided salary progression for employees who chose to remain in the classroom rather than move into managerial posts. This would assist the Department of Education with the recruitment and retention of educators.

signed in the FET College Bargaining Unit of the Education Labour Relations Council (ELRC), recognising college teaching staff who were previously employed by the state as being equal to public school teaching staff and therefore eligible for the occupation-specific dispensation. A further agreement of the ELRC in 2013 (Collective Agreement 2 of 2013) provided for the permanent appointment of temporary and contract staff who had been working at a college for more than 12 months, providing that substantive posts were available. This was immediately followed by Collective Agreement 3 of 2013 which made provision for parity in conditions of service for college lecturers who were still being paid through the state payroll (i.e. formerly employed by the state) and those on college payrolls (i.e. contract teaching staff). This allowed the latter to receive the same benefits as the former. National Treasury had made available R400 million to improve the conditions of service of these contract staff in order to bring them on a par with full-time staff.

Finally, in November 2013, a collective agreement was signed that made way for the transfer of FET college lecturers from the employ of the colleges to the employ of the DHET (i.e. in terms of the Public Service Act), thus giving effect to the FET Colleges Amendment Act of 2012.

Through these various agreements, the DHET has gone some way towards laying the foundation for reversing the effects of the 2006 Act and stabilising the employment conditions in colleges, which seems to have been positively received by college staff. This process will still require a rigorous process of correlating and verifying funded posts against appointments and the payroll, so that the process of migrating staff can be effectively managed.

The shift of the teaching force to the DHET provides the basis for developing an appropriate national plan for human resource development in colleges. Following a five-year protracted process, the DHET has developed a Policy on Professional Qualifications for Lecturers in TVET (RSA, 2013) which details the minimum professional qualification requirements for college lecturers. The FET Summit report from 2010 highlighted the need for a national audit of FET college lecturers. A study by the NBI in 2011 highlighted the complex array of qualifications within the college teaching corps, making it difficult to classify which lecturers would meet the necessary minimum requirements and even more difficult to develop an appropriate intervention plan.

It is clear, however, from the various studies undertaken by the NBI that there is a large number of colleges that lack either the pedagogical or technical knowledge to teach their particular fields of study. There is also generally a poor understanding of the role of the vocational educator and the particular value of the vocational qualification. Furthermore, the various university Schools of Education are ill-equipped to deliver the new vocational educator qualifications and have little track record in training college lecturers. These universities have been wary of taking on the new qualifications, given that the size of the college teaching force is small relative to the public schooling system. The DHET has begun a process to engage universities in the teaching of the new qualifications, but there will be a critical challenge in linking the delivery of these qualifications to a longer-term human resource development strategy for colleges.

Conclusions

The transformation of the FET college sector over the past 20 years has highlighted important lessons for the management of change in a complex and constantly evolving political context. The complexity has its origins in the original formulation of the sector within the constitution as a concurrent national and provincial function (along with public schooling) and separating the sector from the regime which governs training for the workplace. This formulation created a fragmented college system, with few resources and weak support at a provincial level. Until 2009, the college sector limped along, showing little growth and struggling to adapt to the changing policy requirements.

The past few years have seen massive growth, but the DHET has had to expend extensive effort to wrest the colleges away from provinces and reverse some of the key policies that have hampered growth and stability. In doing so, the DHET has consolidated the colleges into a more coherent system and laid the foundation for growth and development.

There are however, a number of critical challenges ahead, some of which have been raised in this chapter. The DHET still needs to make strategic decisions as to which programmes should be grown, rather than further contributing to developing skills for saturated sectors with few employment prospects. The DHET also needs to develop an appropriate plan for college lecturers to ensure that the necessary skills base is in place to deliver on these programmes and ensure students are ready for the workplace. Finally, the DHET needs to ensure that the colleges have the necessary systems in place to responsibly and effectively manage public resources.

More broadly, however, while the DHET has begun to articulate a stronger vision for the college sector, renaming them Technical and Vocational Education and Training (TVET) colleges, the institutions will not be able to live up to this title without being able to occupy a more innovative and responsive space in the education and training market. The extent to which the employability of students is enhanced is dependent on the ability of colleges to produce the right kinds of skills, and on employers being willing to take on students for further training in the workplace.

In taking on these challenges in the next phase of transformation, the critical factor that will ensure success is the creation of a culture of engagement and empowerment within the colleges, so as to create buy-in to government strategy and policy while carefully planning and managing the issues that emerge. In this way, a measure of stability can be maintained while the longer-term challenges are being addressed.

An integrated framework for effective college transformation

Through its work on the Colleges Improvement Project (CIP) in the Eastern Cape and Limpopo, JET developed a comprehensive framework for college improvement (JET, 2012). The fundamental tenet that informed this framework is the need for a transformation approach which not only addresses technical functionality, but also addresses changes in institutional culture, particularly around accountability, responsibility, and professionalism. The framework addressed this at both a strategic and operational level and is ultimately geared to improving the core business of the colleges, which is the student experience.

There are three main pillars of FET college performance.

The first is a high level of administrative efficiency (pillar 3); the second is effective and well-managed efforts to enhance learner performance (pillar 2); and the third is well-planned and well-managed partnerships, and linkages that are productive and are directed at specific learner outcomes (pillar 1). If these areas are effectively managed, the functionality of FET colleges can be improved markedly. The framework is captured in Figure 5.

The most critical pillar – strengthening the various 'functions' in the colleges – is located at the centre of the model. These functions include the core functions of teaching and learning to enhance learner performance and success and all the administrative and corporate service functions which support the process of teaching and learning. If these functions are strengthened, the probability of enhanced college performance is increased significantly.

However, the direct improvement of college functions may not necessarily result in enhanced college functionality. Achieving real and sustainable transformation will depend on change in a number of areas. Based on the CIP's initial assessment of the state of the colleges, the framework identifies six conditions or areas of impact which must be addressed for transformation to be realised. These are outlined below.

Settling outstanding issues

To a greater or lesser extent, each college is plagued with a range of historical conditions which destabilise staff and compromise performance. Some of these conditions are interpersonal issues, and others are related to HR, finance and supply chain management, or stakeholder management. In some circumstances, the presence of these issues may be sufficiently disruptive so as to hinder or constrain any attempt at transformation. This was evident particularly in the Eastern Cape, where colleges were fraught with outstanding issues that were creating high levels of instability and restricted any meaningful attempts at college improvement.

In its first year of operation in the Eastern Cape and Limpopo, JET found that these unresolved issues significantly impeded any meaningful intervention to improve teaching and learning delivery. Similarly, the CIP got swept up in the daily crisis management that resulted from these unresolved issues and found itself being drawn into processes aimed at resolving the issues without having the necessary authority to do so. This situation was alleviated to some extent by the appointment in most of the Eastern Cape colleges of College Administrators who were provided with the relevant authority to tackle outstanding problems and lay the foundation for meaningful change. While placing colleges under administration was not a long-term solution, it demonstrated the importance of applying sufficient pressure to solve outstanding problems.

However, these issues can only be identified and addressed if a systematic diagnosis is conducted on a college by college basis, and the DHET adopts a plan to deal with these issues as a precondition for teaching and learning improvement. The plan must include a bold and proactive approach to utilising the appropriate authority of the state and its officials to directly tackle these outstanding issues as a matter of priority.

FIGURE 5 Integrated Framework **for College Transformation**

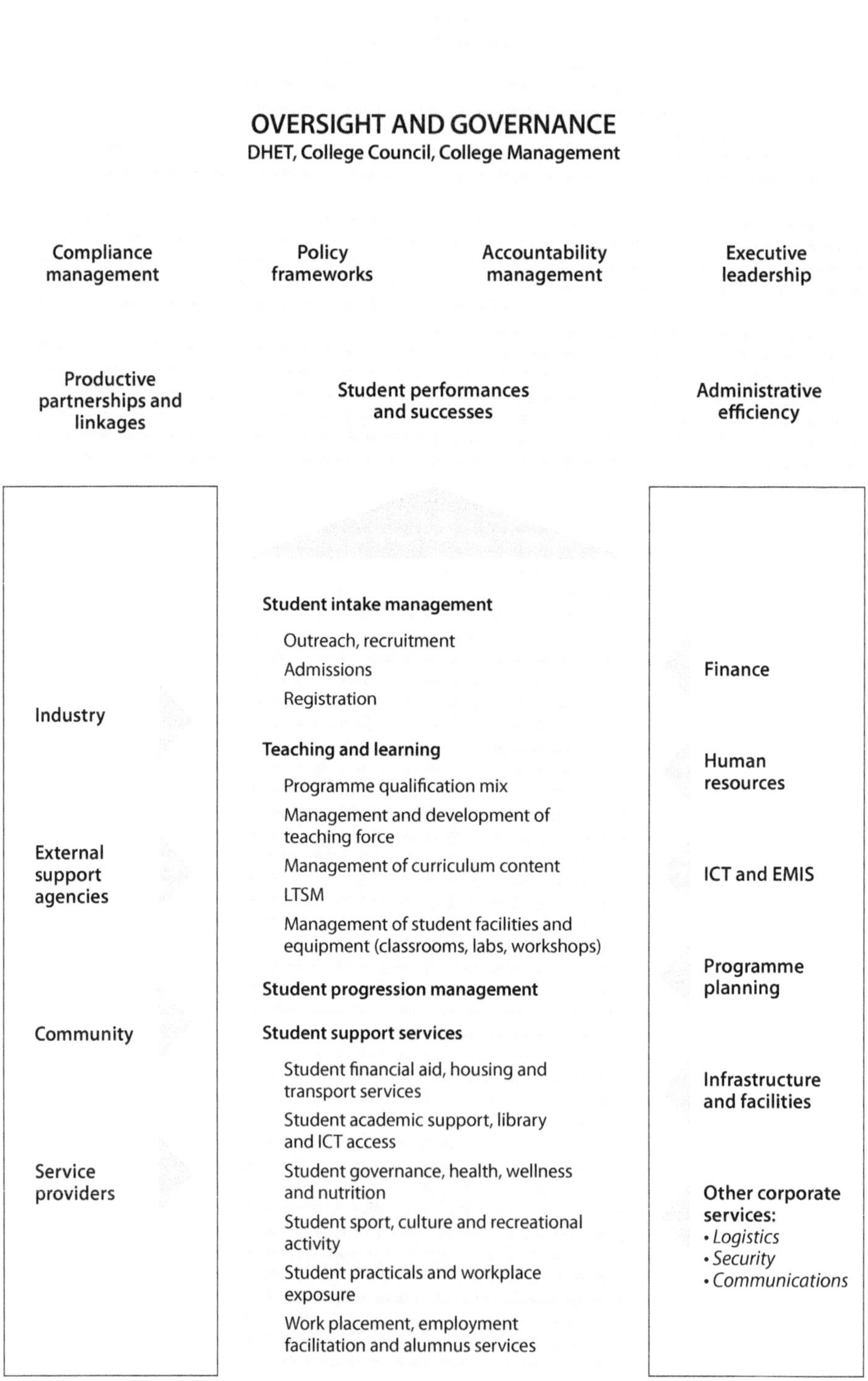

OVERSIGHT AND GOVERNANCE
DHET, College Council, College Management

| Compliance management | Policy frameworks | Accountability management | Executive leadership |

Productive partnerships and linkages — Student performances and successes — Administrative efficiency

Industry	**Student intake management**	Finance
	Outreach, recruitment	
	Admissions	
	Registration	
	Teaching and learning	Human resources
	Programme qualification mix	
External support agencies	Management and development of teaching force	
	Management of curriculum content	ICT and EMIS
	LTSM	
	Management of student facilities and equipment (classrooms, labs, workshops)	
	Student progression management	Programme planning
Community	**Student support services**	
	Student financial aid, housing and transport services	Infrastructure and facilities
	Student academic support, library and ICT access	
Service providers	Student governance, health, wellness and nutrition	Other corporate services:
	Student sport, culture and recreational activity	• Logistics
	Student practicals and workplace exposure	• Security
	Work placement, employment facilitation and alumnus services	• Communications

Strategic alignment

While colleges are all required to undertake strategic planning on an annual basis to comply with public service regulations, this strategic planning is generally not undertaken in a comprehensive and inclusive manner, which undermines the extent to which plans reflect the full scope of the colleges' requirements.

One approach to building the planning function is to ensure that all components of the planning process are undertaken in an efficient and effective manner. Here it is essential to ensure that the responsibility for the leadership and coordination of the planning function is clearly allocated, that distributed responsibilities are assigned, and that critical linkages to budgeting, performance contracting and management, infrastructure planning, HR planning etc. are in place.

During its period of support to colleges' strategic and operational planning in the Eastern Cape and Limpopo, significant improvements were made by the CIP to the quality of plans through focusing on a grounded approach at campus level. Systematic analyses of subject areas identified which areas students were struggling most with and what factors were contributing to this. Plans were then developed to address these factors at a campus level, ultimately correlating the various campus-level interventions into a college-level improvement plan.

For this planning approach to be effective, active buy-in of all concerned and sound leadership to drive the approach were needed. Where strong leadership existed, staff participated actively in, and were committed to realising, the plans. In other instances, the plans were a compliance exercise, and the objectives were not likely to be achieved.

However, due to the particular planning approach that is adopted in colleges, the emphasis remains largely on factors that directly impact on budgets and student performance, and there is limited alignment of the HR, infrastructure, and other related areas. Therefore, there are parts of the colleges that have limited or no involvement in strategic planning, and the strategic objectives of the colleges do not impact on the performance of the individuals concerned. This limits the effectiveness of planning in supporting transformation. A more comprehensive approach to planning is a necessary condition for sustainable college change.

Good governance

Foundations for good governance refer to the policies, agreements, systems, and facilities that are needed in order for a college to operate effectively. The role of the council, the prerogatives of the senior management team, and the obligations and roles of the various units and functions in relation to each other are included.

The appointment of new college councils in 2014, after a protracted vacuum in governance in many colleges, further emphasises the importance of instilling sound governance principles and practices throughout the colleges from the outset. These principles and practices should be embedded in effective governance policies and structures that are seen as legitimate, credible, and authoritative by all in the colleges.

Strengthening functional areas at the colleges

Every college function requires basic resources in order to successfully accomplish its assigned responsibilities. These resources are referred to here as fundamentals for performance and include policies, processes, systems, and capacity. If these are not present, the function will not be able to operate at maximum proficiency. In building college functionality, therefore, it is critical that each of the core college functions be given the best opportunity to successfully deliver on its organisational mandate. This area of impact is most critical in building college functionality, and its concern is that all functions in the college operate at the highest levels of effectiveness and efficiency. The greatest risk to a college is its inability to meet the requisite standards for delivering the quality teaching and learning needed by students and industry.

In its initial conceptualisation of the CIP, JET sought to intervene in each of six functional college areas (Governance and Management, Human Resources, Finance, Planning and Education Management Information Systems, Teaching and Learning, and Student Support) to build policies, processes, systems and capacity.

While functions may be equipped with the necessary resources, the challenge is to ensure these resources are optimised for effective delivery. In the first instance, each function must, within itself, operate in a manner that conforms to standards and expectations. But this is not enough. Functions must also operate in synergy with other functions, if college functionality is to be optimal. This requires a high degree of streamlining, articulation, and integration of responsibilities so that the college functions as a cohesive and responsible unit. All other interventions are intended to ensure that the core functions of the college are properly grounded and are able to operate and generate the highest possible impact for the college.

Building a culture of performance

A culture of performance is the commitment and passion to perform and the drive to attain excellence, not only in one's own function, but for the organisation as a whole. Passion resides in people, and therefore the functionality of colleges must depend on their staff and stakeholders. College functionality will rely not only on peoples' competence and their technical abilities, but on their passion to perform and the overall performance culture in the organisation which drives and feeds that passion. Strengthening an array of organisational functions will only add value if these functions are properly undertaken by people, and only if people are motivated by the culture of performance in the organisation. For this reason, building the culture of performance is considered the catalyst in college functionality.

Achieving measurable and sustainable gains

Each of the conditions outlined above highlights the importance of a systemic and holistic approach to transformation which requires change across the institution as a whole. The complexities associated with such comprehensive change emphasise the fact that such change cannot be achieved very quickly.

In the relatively short period of three years that JET was given to turn colleges in the Eastern Cape and Limpopo around, the intervention was restricted by the level of complexity that underpinned each of the impact areas. While the temptation was to focus solely on impact area 5, there was a strong realisation from the outset that the intervention would be unable to address the functionality of the colleges by focusing on strengthening functions alone.

Ideally, transformation requires a developmental approach – assessing the particular status quo of each college and developing a pathway towards improvement that is particular to the needs of the particular college. The key issue that JET faced was that the developmental approach invariably conflicts with the instability and crisis management that defines the day-to-day operations of the system. Therefore, the challenge for college transformation is how to find a balance between maintaining operational stability and effective teaching and learning, while still implementing a transformational agenda. Considering the scope of change needed, combined with the pressures being placed on colleges to deliver to increasing numbers of youth, the implication is that the realisation of sustainable transformation cannot be achieved in a short period of time, and a more sustained intervention over a longer period of time is needed.

References

Chisholm, L. (1992). *South African technical colleges: Policy options.* Report to National Education Policy Investigation, Human Resource Development Group, University of Durban-Westville and University of Witwatersrand: Education Policy Unit.

Cosser, M., Kraak, A., & Winaar, L. (2011). *Further education and training (FET) colleges at a glance in 2010: FET colleges audit.* Pretoria: Human Sciences Research Council.

Department of Education (DoE). (2003). *Financial and operations procedures toolkit for FET colleges.* Pretoria: Department of Education.

Department of Education (DoE). (2004a). *Linkages & partnerships: An audit.* Pretoria: Department of Education.

Department of Education (DoE). (2004b). *National analysis of financial trends of FET colleges 2000–2002: South Africa.* Pretoria: Department of Education.

Department of Education (DoE). (2004c). *Quantitative overview of the further education and training college sector: A sector in transition.* Pretoria: Department of Education.

Department of Education (DoE). (2008). *National plan for further education and training colleges in South Africa.* Pretoria: Government Printer.

Department of Higher Education and Training (DHET). (2013). *Statistics on post-school education and training in South Africa: 2011.* Pretoria: Department of Higher Education and Training.

Department of Higher Education and Training (DHET). (2014). *Statistics on post-school education and training in South Africa: 2012.* Pretoria: Department of Higher Education and Training.

Fisher, G., Hall, G., & Jaff, R. (1998). *Knowledge and skills for the smart province: A situational analysis of FET institutions in Gauteng.* Johannesburg: National Business Initiative.

Gewer, A. (2005). *Summative evaluation report: Colleges Collaboration Fund 1999–2004.* Johannesburg: JET Education Services.

Gewer, A. (2009). Features of social capital that enhance the employment outcomes of FET college learners. Unpublished PhD Thesis, University of the Witwatersrand.

Gewer, A. (2010). *Choices and chances: FET colleges and the transition from school to work.* Johannesburg: National Business Initiative.

JET Education Services. (2012). *The DHET Eastern Cape FET College Improvement Project intervention design.* Unpublished.

Kraak, A. (2004). Training policies under late apartheid: The historical imprint of a low skill regime. In McGrath, S., Badroodien, A., Kraak, A., & Unwin, L. (Eds), *Shifting understandings of skills in South Africa: Overcoming the historical imprint of a low skills regime.* Cape Town: HSRC Press.

Kraak, A. & Hall, G. (1999). *Transforming further education and training in South Africa: A case study of technical colleges in Kwazulu-Natal.* Pretoria: Human Sciences Research Council.

National Business Initiative (NBI). (1999). *A situational analysis of FET institutions in the Western Cape.* Johannesburg: National Business Initiative.

National Business Initiative (NBI). (2010). *Survey of information technology, construction and engineering lecturers in further education and training colleges.* Johannesburg: National Business Initiative.

National Business Initiative (NBI). (2011). *Lecturer supply, utilisation and development in the further education and training college subsystem.* Johannesburg: National Business Initiative.

National Training Board. (1994). *A national training strategy initiative.* Discussion Document. Pretoria: National Training Board.

Powell, L. & Hall, G. (2002). *Quantitative overview of the further education and training college sector: The New Landscape.* Pretoria: Department of Education.

Republic of South Africa (RSA). (1998a). *Education White Paper 4: A programme for the transformation of further education and training: Preparing for the twenty first century through education, training and work.* Pretoria: Government Printer.

Republic of South Africa (RSA). (1998b). *Further Education and Training Act, No. 98 of 1998.* Pretoria: Government Printer.

Republic of South Africa (RSA). (2006). *Further Education and Training Colleges Act, No. 16 of 2006.* Pretoria: Government Printer.

Republic of South Africa (RSA). (2012). *Further Education and Training Colleges Amendment Act, No. 3 of 2012.* Pretoria: Government Printer.

Republic of South Africa (RSA). (2013). *Policy on professional qualifications for lecturers in technical and vocational education and training.* Pretoria: Government Printer.

Sooklal, S.S. (2004). The structural and cultural constraints on policy implementation: A case study on further education and training colleges in South Africa. Unpublished Doctoral Thesis, University of Pretoria.

chapter 3

THROWING GOOD MONEY AFTER BAD
BARRIERS SOUTH AFRICAN VOCATIONAL TEACHERS EXPERIENCE IN BECOMING COMPETENT EDUCATORS

Ronel Blom
Centre for Research in Education and Labour (REAL),
University of the Witwatersrand

Introduction[10]

In keeping with international trends, the vocational education and training sector in South Africa has been subject to wide-ranging changes in the past 10 to 15 years – not all of which improved the sector. With the introduction of the South African National Qualifications Framework (SANQF) in 1998, technical and vocational education and training (TVET[11]) was earmarked to produce the next generation of skilled workers for the economy, and much effort was put into the reform of this system (see for example Papier, 2010). However, it soon became clear that much of the early policy reform was steeped in symbolism in the form of idealistic statements of intent, which did not necessarily lead to workable and pragmatic approaches to change (Blom, 2006). For example, more than ever before, the South African public TVET college sector became trapped in an education–training divide, quite contrary to the stated ideal of an integrated national system. The divide was keenly felt, particularly by those workers who were denied education and training opportunities under the apartheid regime (Swiss-South African Cooperation Initiative [SSACI], 2010). While an education–training divide is not unique to South Africa (see for example Education International, 2009), in this country, it was strongly associated with the deliberate mediocrity of education for 'non-White' citizens. Parity of esteem between education and training became vested with the ideals for a new system. It was thus with disappointment that it became evident that the public TVET sector had to bear the brunt of a different divide in the post-apartheid era, namely, a fight for turf between two national departments: the Department of Labour (DoL), responsible for sector education and training in workplaces (and the custodian of an enormous source of funds); and the then Department of Education (DoE), responsible for TVET education in public colleges (Heyns & Needham, 2004). The result of this turf war was devastating for colleges – an already diminished apprenticeship system went into further decline; public TVET colleges and workplaces were increasingly de-linked; and outdated vocational education curricula were left unreformed, as these were meant to be replaced by 'learnerships'[12] – a system by now entirely in the hands of Sector Education and Training Authorities (SETAs), in-house and private institutions under the auspices of the DoL. In a short space of time, this situation essentially resulted in two parallel systems: a private TVET system serving the SETAs and the DoL, and a public TVET system under the DoE, experiencing severe contraction and struggling to remain relevant to workplaces and the needs of the economy. In the meantime, the DoE developed and introduced a new 'school-like' vocational curriculum (the NCV), indicated its intent to phase out the old curriculum, and inhibited colleges from offering non-DoE

---

10 This article is based on a paper presented at the Research in Post-Compulsory Education (RCPE) inaugural international research conference of the Further Education Research Association (FERA) held in Oxford, Harris Manchester College, 11–13 July 2014.

11 Until recently (January 2014), with the publication of the White Paper (see reference list), TVET colleges were known as Further Education and Training (FET) colleges.

12 A learnership is a structured learning process for gaining theoretical knowledge and practical skills in the workplace, leading to a nationally recognised qualification. The intention was that learnerships would replace apprenticeships.

programmes through its restrictive funding formulae. To complicate matters further, all of these developments were taking place against the backdrop of general reform impulses in, and reviews and reformulations of, the broader South African system (see for example the report on the review of the SANQF published in 2002 and the subsequent proposed changes to the system published in 2003). Always the last in line in the system, the public TVET college sector again found itself in an untenable position.

With the new cabinet sworn in under President Jacob Zuma in 2009, the DoE was split into two new departments – the Department of Basic Education (DBE), responsible for schooling, and the Department of Higher Education and Training (DHET), now responsible for all post-school education and training, including university education, sector education and training, TVET, and adult education, stripping the DoL of all responsibility for vocational and occupationally directed education and training. The new DHET immediately halted the phasing out of the old curriculum and importantly, became the custodian of the enormous skills development fund amassed by the SETAs. This move was largely supported by the South African education and training community – it was hoped that the divides evident under the previous administration would soon disappear. However, there is now the danger that the new White Paper for Post-school Education and Training's (DHET, 2013) ambitions may also be un-implementable, as the sector looked upon to develop key mid-level skills for the economy and enhance employment is considered to be the weakest sector in the system.

Nevertheless, since 2009, there has been an unprecedented focus on the public TVET sector in the country. Apart from the systemic problems in terms of the contested turf noted above, this move seems to have been motivated by a number of drivers: the massive (and growing) unemployment rate of youth (especially black youth) who exit formal schooling prior to achieving a school-leaving certificate; the struggling economy; the need to (re)industrialise the economy of South Africa; and, possibly, the deeply held (but contested) belief that there is a relationship between vocational education and the revitalisation of the economy.

These dynamics are mirrored throughout the world, and have been shown in sharp relief since the economic downturn of 2008. National and international policy reforms are placing the burden of an economic turnaround strategy on the TVET systems of the world – 'skills for sustainable growth' has become the international mantra (see for example the World Bank, 2010; ILO, 2011; OECD, 2010; UNESCO, 2012).

Yet, in the second term of President Jacob Zuma's cabinet, and despite massive injections of funds to recapitalise and capacitate the sector (Papier, 2010), the weakest link in these ambitions is still the capacity of vocational education educators to deal with the pressures brought to bear on them. This seems to be because policy reforms often disregard the people who have to implement the ambitions expressed. In the TVET sector, it is not simply a matter of updating pedagogical practice and/or subject matter expertise (even though these matters also need attention). It has emerged that current conditions of service and the casualisation of work in general have had a major impact on TVET teachers' motivation to learn and to update their skills to meet the additional demands. Further, TVET teachers' perceived low status and the lack of a professional identity, compounded by apathy of institutional managers and restrictive funding regimes, seem to exacerbate the situation. These problems emerge only when 'reading between the lines' of the numerous reports[13] submitted to the DHET.

As elsewhere in the world (see for example Keep, 2007), the South African government has responded to the triple challenge of unemployment, a failing economy, and reindustrialisation by proposing education and training policy and by conceptualising qualifications for vocational educators, in the hope that policy will serve as a trigger to becoming more responsive to the needs of the economy through the development of more skilled educators. While these policy impulses will undoubtedly be necessary at some point, in the short to medium term it may not be the most urgent, or the most effective, of interventions in the college sector. Instead, the daily struggles of vocational educators present some of the more immediate inhibitors for change.

This article will therefore interrogate the non-academic, i.e. the non-subject-matter, barriers that South African vocational teachers experience in becoming competent educators able to meet the expressed needs. It does so by analysing a number of high-level reports submitted to the DHET over the past three to four years in respect of public TVET colleges. Many of the reports were compiled in preparation of the new White Paper for Post-School Education and Training (DHET, 2013), or as inputs to the National Development Plan (NDP),[14] and highlight general and specific problems of the sector. The analysis was supported by three exploratory interviews with high-ranking people working in the sector,[15] with the intention of delving into all possible factors which may impact vocational teachers' capacity and formulating research questions for further studies.

Reading between the lines

The DHET's Green Paper for Post-School Education and Training (DHET, 2012: 20) stated that 'there are high expectations of [the public TVET] sector as a central component of South Africa's skills development system', but in the same document, admitted that 'most of our colleges are weak institutions'. In the introduction to this article one of these weaknesses was alluded to: inadequate subject expertise of TVET teachers. Further, the Green Paper also mentions poor management capacity and financial management and a poor understanding by TVET teachers of workplace environments and requirements (DHET, 2012). Added to these is the lack of the knowledge (and practice) of pedagogy appropriate to vocational education (Mokone, 2011). These issues are by no means minor, stemming partly from the troubled history of the sector. However, there seems to be more to the sector's problems than subject knowledge and managerial capacities.

---

13 These reports were compiled in anticipation of the new White Paper for Post-school Education and Training (see references list).

14 The National Development Plan (2011) is an ambitious plan compiled by the National Planning Commission appointed by the President to address the numerous economic, social and educational problems experienced in South Africa.

15 The first respondent is a senior member of staff at a non-government organisation (NGO) involved with capacity building in the TVET sector on behalf of the Quality Council for Trades and Occupations (QCTO) (PC1); the second is the Chairperson of the QCTO (PC2); and the third is an academic and ex-lecturer from a TVET college (PC3). Information from these individuals is referenced as PC (personal communication): PC1, PC2, or PC3.

In respect of subject expertise and vocational pedagogy, current staff have very different levels and types of qualifications, ranging from those with formal teaching qualifications or degrees to those with trade qualifications/trade theory qualifications or industry credentials, but no teaching expertise, and vice versa:

> *Lecturers with industry experience have practical skills of workshop training but lack theoretical knowledge for classroom teaching, whereas lecturers from teaching backgrounds have theoretical knowledge for classroom teaching but lacked practical experience for workshop training. (Mokone, 2011: 28)*

Taylor (2011: 47) adds that until recently,[16] in South Africa 'there was no training base for FET college lecturers, and no new qualifications framework as yet for lecturing staff', which means that current teaching staff come from very different traditions and have very different skills.

Again, this situation is not unique to South Africa. At a United Nations Educational, Scientific and Cultural Organisation (UNESCO) conference in 2012 the participants noted that:

> *Existing [education] systems generally tend to provide the same pre-service training preparation for TVET teachers as received by their counterparts across the wider field of teaching. Moreover, many TVET teachers enter the classroom without the benefit of an industrial background, and having often lacked the opportunity to experience the world of work. (UNESCO, 2012: 5)*

While it is comforting for South African commentators to know that TVET teachers all over the world seem to be in the same boat, and that our own national department has recognised the need for targeted education and training through its development of a suite of qualifications appropriate for TVET teaching (see RSA, 2013), these factors are not the only problems besetting the sector. It is therefore surprising that despite the stated centrality of the TVET sector for post-school education in terms of 'the development of a skilled and educated population [and] for meeting the needs of an economy which suffers a serious shortage of mid-level skills' (DHET, 2013: 11), other possible reasons for the problems experienced by the TVET sector in South Africa are glossed over in the Green Paper (2012). Further, the Green Paper limits its comments to issues of conditions of employment, and no problems other than the general problems already noted are mentioned at all in the subsequent White Paper (DHET, 2013).

It is therefore only when 'reading between the lines' that the diversity of qualifications held by TVET teachers is seen to contribute to capacity-building barriers. Further, when a weak training base is combined with the poor conditions of service, demanding college programmes, the sociological context of students, and a restrictive funding model, it is a serious oversight to dismiss these problems, which may critically inhibit the capacity-

---

16 A suite of qualifications aimed at the development of TVET college lecturers was proposed in 2013.

building and expansion plans for the sector. In the sections following, each of these factors will be discussed.

Diversity and levels of current TVET teacher qualifications

In order for school teachers in South Africa to be registered with the South African Council for Educators (SACE), they have to successfully complete a four-year Bachelor of Education (BEd) degree. Even allowing for differences in the quality of programmes offered by autonomous universities, the BEd can be considered the minimum standard to be achieved before entering the teaching profession. Until very recently, with the publication of a suite of TVET teacher qualifications (2013), no such minimum standard existed for TVET teachers in South Africa. Furthermore, these new standards have not yet been implemented, and current college staff qualifications therefore represent a hodgepodge of programmes which cannot be considered to be at the same or similar levels – either with each other, or with the BEd school teacher qualification. The situation is depicted in the following figure. For example, in 2011, there were 15 526 TVET teachers in the system, with at least 25 different types of qualifications.[17]

FIGURE 6 Number and types of TVET college teacher qualifications (2011)

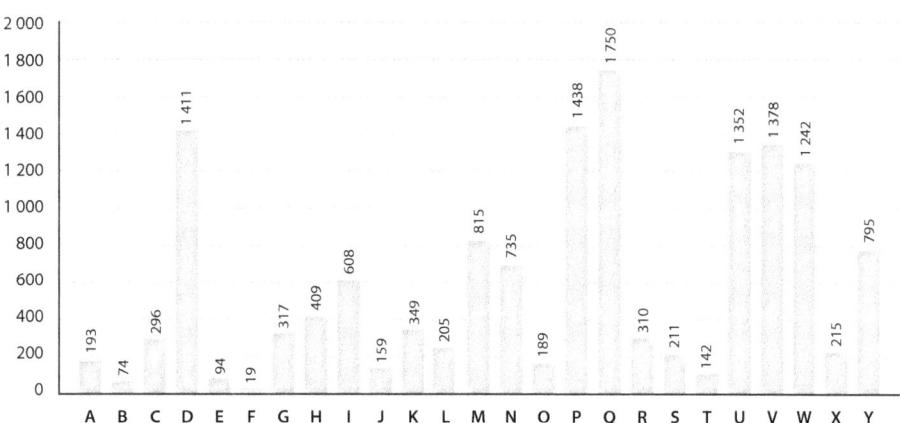

Source: DHET (2011).

The National N3 to N6 qualification is shown by Q (1 750) in the figure, the National (N) Diploma by P (1 438), and artisanal qualifications by D (1 411). These represent the qualifications of those TVET teachers who have completed a college programme and have either returned or stayed on as teachers at the college, but who have neither been trained as teachers nor, in many cases, had workplace experience. These programmes are considered particularly outdated and weak, yet this is the largest group in the cohort.

---

17 Unverified data from a database that the DHET developed of lecturer qualifications in 2011. According to PC3, the data is unverified as lecturers were reluctant to confirm or disagree out of fear that their conditions of service may be affected.

The Education Diploma/National Professional Diploma in Education shown by V (1 378) is a school teaching programme, at one time offered to school teachers with outdated teaching qualifications and now discontinued – the last cohort was enrolled in 2014.

The Bachelor degree, U (1 352), does not include teaching expertise, while the National Diploma, W (1 242), is a technical/occupation-directed programme offered by the former technikons,[18] also with no teaching focus.

M, the Higher Diploma in Education and the Post-Graduate Certificate in Education (815), and I, the Higher Diploma in Education (608) are school teaching qualifications offered prior to the introduction of the BEd, all of which have also long since been discontinued.

N (735) represents a combination of postgraduate degrees and reflects the change in the system when the BEd degree was first introduced as the minimum standard. Many TVET teachers still hold only these qualifications.

G (317), the Bachelor of Technology, and J (159), the National Higher Diploma, are also programmes offered by the former technikons. They are technical and/or occupationally orientated programmes, but here, also, do not include training as a TVET teacher.

C (296), L (250), R (310), S (211), T (142), and X (215) are mostly school teacher upgrading qualifications introduced over the years, or school teacher programmes that have been adapted to a vocational education focus, often also offered by the former technikons.

A small group of university graduates, H (409), also teach at colleges, again without teaching expertise. An equally small group, A (193) and B (74), excluding the doctoral and master's graduates (19 and 189 respectively), have an adult teaching qualification.

Another 795, shown by Y, have a partially completed qualification or no qualification beyond the school-leaving certificate.

In the personal communications with the first interviewee (PC1), the ways in which this situation plays itself out in terms of capacity building in the sector became evident. PC1 indicated that the people with degrees and teaching qualifications, despite not having much occupational workplace experience, feel that they do not need additional capacity building as they are achieving relatively good results in their subject areas (PC1). Furthermore, they are usually those TVET teachers who are offering the 'school-like' basic Sciences, English, or Mathematics (Education International, 2009).

However, with the group comprising Q, P, D and W (a total of 5 841 TVET college teachers), a number of issues emerge. Firstly, the current qualifications of these teachers do not provide them with access to higher education without them having to undertake substantial additional work before they can embark on undergraduate training. Secondly, their own learning trajectories of having achieved their qualifications at colleges means that they are not academically inclined anyway, so the 'jump is too big, too onerous, and the demands are too high' (PC1). Furthermore, as PC2 indicated, they see themselves not as teachers first, but as 'technical' practitioners – they therefore place more value on their industry backgrounds (if they have any) than on teaching, reflecting their lack of

---

18 Similar to polytechnics – they have now been converted to universities of technology.

professional identity as TVET teachers (PC2). This group is also most likely in their 50s, and they therefore come from a 'technical college'[19] background, which offered only those low-status, low-value qualifications that existed prior to the introduction of a new curriculum. Consequently, these teachers tend to struggle to come to terms with the demands of the new curriculum (PC2). PC1 was also of the opinion that they may be 'afraid to expose their own weaknesses and incompetence in terms of teaching', so they avoid any development that may 'show them up' (PC1). Finally, in respect of this group, PC3 suggested that there are no financial incentives for teachers to take on personal and professional development, and that higher education institutions, in any case, have not been offering programmes that are appropriate for vocationally orientated teaching (PC3). PC2 agreed and indicated that whereas in school teaching there is a clear trajectory of promotion through the ranks, in the college sector this kind of trajectory is weak or non-existent (PC2), which leads us to the next underlying problem: conditions of service.

Conditions of service

The extent to which the constant policy churn has impacted on the motivation and morale of TVET teachers cannot be overemphasised. In a short space of time, the sector and staff have had to accommodate sweeping changes, some of which included the conditions of service of staff. For example, prior to the introduction of the FET Act No. 16 of 2006, colleges were a 'provincial competence' – in other words, management and staff were appointed by provincial departments of education. However, with the promulgation of the 2006 FET Act, TVET teaching staff were to be appointed by college councils. In the words of the 2012 Green Paper this change has had 'many unintended consequences':

> *One was that the change of employer from the state to the College Councils caused an exodus of around 12% of college lecturers who did not have confidence in their council as an employer and preferred to stay in the employment of the state. Another is a tendency for college staff to be hired on short-term contracts, aligned to learner enrolment for specific short-term programmes. This is clearly contrary to any notion of long-term professional development for lecturers. (DHET, 2012: 25)*

Subsequent to these moves, and in terms of the amended FET Act (as amended in 2012 in accordance with the Further Education and Training Laws Amendment Act No. 3 of 2012), TVET colleges became a 'national competence', directly under the auspices of the DHET, which again meant a change in management of the sector. Further, as noted earlier, the conditions of service do not appear to have been considered in the FET White Paper (DHET, 2013), suggesting perhaps that the problems outlined above had been dealt with in the intervening year. Furthermore, apart from the devastating loss of staff

---

19 TVET colleges were known as 'technical colleges' prior to the introduction of the Further Education and Training Act in 2006, after which they were known as FET colleges – this is in itself indicative of the turbulent policy changes in the sector. Now, they have been renamed again as Technical and Vocational Education and Training (TVET) colleges.

due to the introduction of the FET Act in 2006, the problem of replacing experienced staff leaving the sector has been exacerbated by the fact that no pipeline of new TVET teachers is being developed. This means that once again, colleges have been forced to appoint their own graduates who do not have the requisite qualifications or experience, neither in terms of subject matter and teaching expertise, nor in terms of workplace experience.

In addition, both PC1 and PC3 confirmed, in particular, that the short-term nature of teaching positions has hardly changed (PC1 and PC2). The consequence of the casualisation of TVET teachers' work is that college management is reluctant to develop staff on short-term contracts, which, in the opinion of PC2 reflects the lack of a culture of development and staff capacity building in the sector (PC2). Likewise, TVET college teachers themselves seem to be too anxious about their precarious position to concern themselves with training: the teachers who are on short-term contracts 'are always seeking permanent employment opportunities' and feel that they cannot 'focus on their teaching' (Mokone, 2011: 13). Further, given the distrust that seems to exist between staff and management, staff feel that if they undertake training, the 'college owns you' (PC3); they consider themselves obligated to stay in the service of the college when they have undergone training and development. This attitude is clearly in contravention of the intentions of the DHET namely, 'to improve the qualifications and capabilities of college lecturers' (DHET, 2013: 17) and is counter-productive in terms of improving teaching and learning at TVET colleges. Colleges are generally also not in a position to undertake internal training and development, and where training does take place, there seems to be a mismatch between what TVET teachers feel they need and what they are offered:

> *The perception is that management ... force lecturers to attend these programmes as most of them are not what lecturers identified as part of their training and developmental needs. Therefore, the prevailing view is that FET college management imposes the academic development training on them. (Mokone, 2011: 15)*

The type of training offered is also often seen as inappropriate for the college environment: 'assessor and moderator courses are not linked to the learning programmes [that they are teaching]' (Mokone, 2011: 11).

This situation impacts directly on the next emerging theme.

Demands of TVET college programmes

It is when the aspirations articulated by the DHET for the TVET sector and the reality on the ground are compared that it becomes evident how far the system still has to go: while 'Government expects that TVET colleges will become the cornerstone of the country's skills development system. Thus, a major effort will be made to increase enrolments' (DHET, 2013: 12), it is recognised that 'the mix of qualifications in TVET colleges is complex to administer, difficult for learners and parents to understand, and often poorly quality assured' (DHET, 2013: 14). Nevertheless, despite the acknowledgement of problems in the sector, PC1 was adamant that 'the sense created is that everything can be introduced into the colleges'. Thus, on the one hand the colleges are seen to be the solution to the country's skills development shortages, but on the other, there is the recognition that all is not well in the colleges.

Moreover, when these expectations are coupled with a variety of funding streams, which often drive implementation of new programmes (more about funding later), TVET teachers seem to be very poorly prepared to deal with all the expectations. For example, PC1 noted, as an ex-TVET teacher herself, that 'we had five days of training to introduce a whole new curriculum', and 'subject matter support was not forthcoming'. This situation is confirmed by the requests for training and development, particularly in respect of the use of workshop equipment associated with the new curriculum:

> *Lecturers reported that they [have never had] training on how to use new equipment that [was] purchased during the recapitalisation of FET colleges. As a result some of the workshops have modernised resources but are not fully utilized. Some lecturers cannot operate new machines which have been at FET colleges for five years ... (Mokone, 2011: 16)*

The new 'school-like' curriculum, the National Certificate Vocational (NCV), introduced in 2007 under the DoE, was so different from the previous programmes taught, that many TVET teachers have taken a long time to adjust to a new and very full programme (PC2). Furthermore, teachers are often expected to teach the old curriculum as well as the new, and management seems to deploy teachers interchangeably between these curricula, each of which have different assessment, quality assurance, and teaching demands (PC3). Indeed, the different curricula represent different cohorts of students – those who have dropped out of school early (at Grade 9), and those who have completed schooling (Grade 12). Often these students would be grouped in one class.

PC3 was particularly vocal on the demands of the new curriculum, for two reasons: she maintains that due to the number of occupational specialisations associated with the new curriculum, TVET teachers are often required to teach disciplines which fall outside their subject matter expertise, and this situation seems to be exacerbated by the fact that the teachers often do not have the pedagogical knowledge to assist in switching between disciplines.

Even more seriously, it seems that lecturers dislike this curriculum because they feel that there are currently no clear articulation routes for further study for students completing these programmes. PC3 claimed that TVET teachers feel that 'they are babysitting the students on this NCV curriculum' for the time that they are at the college, because it 'takes them nowhere'; and that college management feels 'there is nothing they can do' to improve the situation because funding is linked to this programme. The historic weaknesses of the TVET sector are therefore simply perpetuated, and the capacity-building interventions so far seem to have been inappropriate and ineffectual (PC1).

Three additional matters which are linked to the demands of TVET college programmes, but not necessarily to a particular curriculum, are important to raise: the language of teaching and learning; multi-level, multi-grade teaching; and overcrowding due to rapid expansion in student numbers.

Firstly, PC3 made the point that 'we believe in the myth that students who come to the college can cope in academic studies'. This can't be further from the truth. Even under the previous dispensation, prior to the introduction of the recent policy reforms and the new curriculum, the students who attended colleges were, more often than not, redirected out of mainstream, academic schools to 'go and learn a trade'. Now, with greatly expanding enrolments amongst all race groups, more of the so-called weaker students are directed out of mainstream schools, where the language of teaching and learning has become a significant barrier to success. PC3 noted that 'students often only encounter English at school'. As a result, in most colleges, staff and students are teaching and learning in a second or third language. Poor command of English, especially of those TVET teachers who come from industry, affect their understanding and utilisation of textbooks (which are also only available in English) and their teaching (PC3). The result is that teachers teach only those students who seem to be able to cope with learning in English (PC3).

Secondly, when the new curriculum was introduced, 'it was originally meant for young people [who have completed] Grade 9' (DHET, 2013: 14), but due to confusing admission policies, TVET colleges admitted students to this programme who had completed Grade 12 (the school-leaving year). Apart from the fact that colleges soon found that students who have finished Grade 12 are in a much better position to cope with the demands of the programme, classes are often made up of multi-level, multi-grade students, placing even more pressure on TVET teachers to deal with different cohorts in one class (Mokone, 2011).

Thirdly, the DHET has been very successful in expanding enrolments at TVET colleges, both through enrolment targets and student funding:

> Head-count enrolments increased from 345 566 in 2010 to an estimated 650 000 in 2013; enrolments are expected to increase to one million by 2015 ... (DHET, 2013: 13)

Therefore, in addition to classroom pedagogy and, in many cases, workplace experience, TVET teachers are calling for 'skills to manage workshops and overcrowding in the classrooms' (Mokone, 2011: 15).

Further, given that many of the students have been redirected out of academic schools due to their poor performance, TVET teachers have to deal with the sociological issues of this student body.

The sociological demands of students

TVET teachers, when asked about whether they see teaching as a 'calling', indicated that in the past, college students were more 'mature and responsible' (Mokone, 2011), and that they enjoyed teaching the students. However, with the introduction of the new curriculum and the redirection of more of the weaker school students to colleges, TVET teachers now deal with adolescents, rather than with young adults (Mokone, 2011), and find these students 'ill-disciplined' and 'lacking in motivation' (Mokone, 2011). TVET teachers also find that the students become demotivated due to their failure to progress and then lose interest in learning. The TVET teachers do not know how to deal with the students' issues (Mokone, 2011). They partly blame this on the communities' lack of understanding of TVET and poor career counselling, both at school and prior to admission to college (Mokone, 2011). Furthermore, given the poor pass rates, many TVET teachers seem to feel that 'there should be a bridging course to assist learners to cope with the demands of the [programme]' (Mokone, 2011: 12). TVET teachers are therefore of the opinion that many students have serious problems in adapting to college life:

> *Complaints were raised that learners do not submit class work and [homework], [they] come late, [and there is] no accountability, [as] learners are allowed to write examinations even if they do not have the required entrance examination marks. (Mokone, 2011: 13)*

Apart from the waste this represents in terms of financial resources, students also have learning difficulties which are hard to deal with in the context of the current teaching loads and overcrowding (Mokone, 2011). Consequently, TVET teachers suggested that they need training and development in respect of (in no particular order)

> *teaching methodologies, communication management, financial management, accounting management, conflict management, project management, office practice, adult and multicultural teaching, team building, student and classroom management and leadership. (Mokone, 2011: 14)*

In addition, they indicated that they need (again, not in any particular order) training in

> *office data processing, use of overhead and data projectors, how to use modern equipment in workshops, research skills, computer literacy, implementation of [the curriculum], compilation of learning materials, educational psychology, teaching skills ... (Mokone, 2011: 16)*

To date, the training and development needs do not seem to match what has been offered. When these factors are combined with disincentives created by the current funding regimes, then the situation becomes critical.

Funding

Funding influences everything in public TVET colleges in South Africa. In most cases, colleges have two or more funding streams: funding in respect of the old curriculum, and separately, funding for the new curriculum; then they often receive funding in respect of the SETA learnerships; and finally, funding is provided for short-term projects, often from foreign donors (PC1). In the light of these funding streams, it is not surprising that TVET teachers are calling for financial, accounting, and project management in addition to teaching and classroom management training. However, the funding model itself may also inadvertently inhibit colleges from introducing innovative programmes, especially programmes that may provide articulation routes for the new curriculum, which could solve the 'baby-sitting' problem (PC3). This situation arises because such articulation programmes are unfunded, despite the DHET's encouragement to implement them:

Recently Level 5 (Higher Certificate) programmes have been introduced in some colleges in partnership with universities. This has worked well in terms of developing and enhancing intermediate skills which are in high demand. These programmes are often occupationally directed but have strong articulation possibilities into higher education ... (DHET, 2013: 15)

However, PC3, in working with some of these colleges attempting to introduce Higher Certificates, maintains that TVET colleges 'refuse to market programmes that have no funding associated with them'. This means that in addition to a lack of articulation with higher education for students, collaboration with university teachers to improve the subject matter expertise of TVET teachers is discouraged by the lack of funding.

Another consequence of the current funding model is that colleges are concerned with enrolment numbers and not with the appropriate selection of students for particular programmes (PC3), with the result that even greater demands are made on TVET teachers. For example, colleges enrol students for programmes without regard to whether the students need a firm basis in mathematics or not. It is only after enrolment that teachers for Financial Accounting, Information Technology and Engineering programmes, for example, discover the students' deficiencies in the basics.

Nevertheless, the DHET (2013) is adamant that the TVET college sector should be responsible for the development of mid-level skills for the economy, and consequently the college sector is targeted for the greatest expansion in the post-school system. The rapid increase in enrolments is raising concerns about 'further diluting the quality' of teaching and learning in the colleges (PC1) and the 'lack of accountability' in respect of the funding. PC3, for example, indicated that no questions are asked about the poor throughput and pass rates, which means that TVET teachers (and students) do not learn from the assessment of their students; all funding is in relation to enrolment targets. She believes that this approach will bring about 'reproductions of poverty', as the success of students is far from a priority. Students consequently leave the colleges without being prepared either for further learning, or for work (PC3).

Conclusion

In South Africa, as elsewhere in the world, TVET is seen to be an increasingly important element of the education and training system. Countries respond to this imperative in many different ways. The South African government has chosen to respond by completely reorganising the post-school education and training sector, developing new policies, and rearranging the management of the sector. It remains to be seen how successful this realignment will be, but even the best plans will fail if there is poor recognition of what the situation on the ground may be. In this regard, some serious questions should be raised about the ambitions of the White Paper (DHET, 2013) in respect of its expansion plans for the TVET sector. This is because much of what is expressed in the White Paper can be considered to be political symbolism (Jansen, 2002), namely that policies are often developed as a symbol of change, rather than with an intention to really effect change:

The policy literature in developing countries is replete with narratives of 'failure'

> attributed to the lack of resources, the inadequacy of teacher training, the weak
> design of implementation strategy, and the problems of policy coherence. This
> research on education policymaking after apartheid presents the following puzzle:
> what if the impressive policies designed to change apartheid education did not
> have 'implementation' as their primary commitment? (Jansen, 2002: 199)

Nevertheless, in the past three years alone, bursary allocation to students increased from R300 million in 2010 to R1.988 billion in 2013 (DHET, 2013). While it is laudable that students from poor families are not only given bursaries for class fees, but also for transport and accommodation, this indiscriminate expansion in student enrolments is placing a huge burden on an already weak and poorly managed sector. The sheer pressure of student numbers will render policies ineffectual if concurrent improvements are not made in respect of TVET teachers themselves by seriously paying attention to their concerns.

As can be seen from the mixed bag of current qualifications, the upgrading of qualifications and the capacity of TVET teachers to teach in diverse settings needs serious attention. However, the introduction of appropriate qualifications is not enough – which at any rate will take a number of years to introduce, and more years still to develop a new pipeline of TVET teachers.

The stabilisation of staff conditions of employment is therefore paramount. At the moment, this situation plays itself out in the lack of trust between staff and management. This situation is also likely to discourage new recruits to the profession, and it may therefore be difficult to develop a pipeline of TVET teachers.

However, the two most important (short-term) interventions seem to hinge on the immediate needs of TVET teachers to better interpret and understand the current curricula they are teaching, and the need for TVET teachers to learn how to deal with some of the debilitating sociological problems experienced by students. In no small measure, the under-preparedness of students seems to be linked to TVET teachers' sense of helplessness which could lead to their lack of motivation for self-development.

In short, apart from improving management at colleges (clearly articulated in the White Paper) (DHET, 2013), TVET institutions need to be strengthened in terms of their capacity to meet the needs of teachers and students. Finally, since TVET colleges are known for the fact that they only promote programmes that are linked to funding, a more equitable and diverse funding regime needs to be considered.

Sadly, linked to indiscriminate funding is the poor selection of students. Colleges often discover later that they have oversubscribed certain programmes, purely for the sake of attaining the maximum funding for enrolments. The result is not only that classrooms and/or workshops are uncomfortably full, but the success rates of students at colleges are notoriously poor. The massive injection of funds and the direction of these funds to bursaries and subsidies to offer programmes regardless of whether students are succeeding may indeed be a case of throwing good money after bad.

What universities can do

In the international literature, there are debates about TVET teacher training. On the one hand, UNESCO recommends that the training of TVET teachers should 'preferably be offered as a tertiary programme', combined with various in-service and lifelong learning programmes (UNESCO, 2001: 81–87, cited in Education International, 2009: 16). Furthermore, the view is that TVET teacher training should be longer than training for school teachers 'due to the requirement for the TVET teacher to have practical experience' (UNESCO, 1973: 98, cited in Education International, 2009: 17). On the other hand, the Organisation for Economic Cooperation and Development (OECD) recommends that the 'pedagogical requirements should be lower', especially if TVET teachers are recruited from industry (OECD, 2009: 34, cited in Education International, 2009: 17). Grollman and Rauner (2007) call this 'a fundamental dilemma between recruitment of TVET teachers and the practices of TVET teaching and learning':

> *There is either, on the one hand, a highly professionalised model of teacher education and recruitment associated with a strong alienation from the world of work, [and] on the other hand an ad hoc-type model of recruitment based on experience in the field, leading to occupational localism or strong subject-based identities. (Grollman & Rauner, 2007, cited in Education International, 2009: 17)*

For South Africa this is an important caution to keep in mind when specific qualifications for TVET teachers are introduced from 2016/17. The DHET has published a suite of qualifications intended to accommodate various entrance, articulation, and upgrading routes. These qualifications provide for pre-service, but also in-service, development, especially for those TVET teachers already in the system. By providing alternative pathways into higher education there is also the recognition that many current TVET teachers may not meet the minimum entry requirements for Bachelor degrees. A further important element is the substantial work-integrated learning (WIL) component in all of the qualifications. This is in keeping with the DHET's intention to prioritise workplace experience of TVET teachers: 'to ensure that their training is up to date with workplace needs of employers in their field' (DHET, 2013: 17). Universities will therefore play an increasingly important role in the development and capacity building of the pipeline of TVET teachers, as well as in the upgrading of the current cadre of teachers in the sector.

However, responding with a suite of qualifications addresses only part of the problem, as can be seen in the previous discussions. Developing qualifications will not magically encourage and motivate TVET teachers to embark on study.

Research

Universities are responsible for the development of new bodies of knowledge. Internationally, there has been much research undertaken in respect of vocational pedagogy, but in South Africa this is a relatively new field of inquiry (Papier, 2013). In the development of qualifications for upgrading of the current cadre of TVET teachers and for a new pipeline of TVET teachers, vocational pedagogy is important and should inform the curricula of TVET teacher qualifications. However, it is also clear that TVET teachers' work is not only about the enactment of a particular curriculum using appropriate pedagogies – there seem to be a number of other factors which influence their work. The persistent poor performance of the TVET sector in South Africa suggests that a deeper investigation into the reasons for these weaknesses is needed. Given that the sector carries the burden of the expectations of the system, a study of the context, hopes, and fears of TVET teachers is important. Hopefully, this will end the indiscriminate pouring of money into a system which is ill-prepared to make the best use of it.

Acknowledgements

The research, of which this article forms a part, is funded by the National Department of Higher Education and Training of South Africa. The Department has no involvement in the study.

References

Blom, J.P. (2006). The ideal of an integrated national qualifications framework. Unpublished thesis. University of Pretoria.

Department of Higher Education and Training (DHET). (2011). Database of lecturer qualifications in 2011 (unverified).

Department of Higher Education and Training (DHET). (2012). *Green paper for post-school education and training: The doors of learning and culture shall be opened.* Pretoria: Department of Higher Education and Training.

Department of Higher Education and Training (DHET). (2013). *White paper for post-school education and training: Building an expanded, effective and integrated post-school system.* Pretoria: Department of Higher Education and Training.

Education International. (2009). *Literature review: Vocational education and training.* Brussels: Education International. Retrieved from http://www.ei-ie.org/, January 2014.

Grint, K. (2005). *The sociology of work.* Cambridge, UK: Polity Press.

Heyns, R. & Needham, S. (2004). An integrated national framework for education and training in South Africa: Exploring the issues. *South African Qualifications Authority Bulletin,* 6(2): 30–48.

International Labour Office (ILO). (2011). *A skilled workforce for strong, sustainable and balanced growth. A G20 training strategy.* Geneva: International Labour Office.

Jansen, J.D. (2002). Political symbolism as policy craft: Explaining non-reform in South African education after apartheid. *Journal of Education Policy,* 17(2): 199–215.

Keep, E. (2007). State control of the English education and training system – playing with the biggest train set in the world. *Journal of Vocational Education and Training,* 58(1): 47–64.

Mokone, K. (2011). *The impact of academic development programmes on the performance of lecturers in the classroom at public further education and training colleges.* Retrieved from http://www.sadtu.org.za/, January 2014.

Organisation for Economic Cooperation and Development (OECD). (2010). *Learning for jobs. Synthesis report of the OECD reviews of vocational education and training.* Paris: Organisation for Economic Cooperation and Development (OECD) Publishing. http//dx.doi.org/10.1787/9789264214682-en.

Papier, J. (2010). From policy to curriculum in South African vocational teacher education: A comparative perspective. *Journal of Vocational Education and Training,* 62(2): 153–162.

Papier, J. (2013). What are we learning about vocational teacher education? Presentation to the VET-NET colloquium hosted by the Centre for Researching Education and Labour. *Pedagogy for Technical and Vocational Education,* University of Johannesburg, 26 November 2013.

Republic of South Africa (RSA), Department of Education (DoE) and Department of Labour (DoL). (2002). *Report of the study team on the implementation of the national qualifications framework.* Pretoria: Department of Education and Department of Labour.

Republic of South Africa (RSA), Department of Education (DoE) and Department of Labour (DoL), (2003). *An interdependent national qualifications framework system. Consultative document.* Pretoria: Department of Education and Department of Labour.

Republic of South Africa (RSA). (2013). Policy on professional qualifications for lecturers in technical and vocational education and training. *Government Gazette,* 576(36554), 11 June 2013. Pretoria: South Africa.

Swiss-South African Cooperation Initiative (SSACI). (2010). *Report of the further education and training steering committee. Recommendations to the Minister of Higher Education and Training.* Retrieved from http://www.ssaci.org.za/, March 2014.

Taylor, N. (2011). *Priorities for addressing South Africa's education and training crisis. A review commissioned by the National Planning Commission.* Retrieved from http://www.jet.org.za/, March 2014.

World Bank. (2010). *Stepping up skills for more jobs and higher productivity.* Washington, DC: World Bank.

United Nations Educational, Scientific and Cultural Organisation (UNESCO). (2012). *Strengthening TVET teacher education.* Report of the UNESCO-UNEVOC online conference, 25 June to 6 July 2012. Retrieved from http://www.unevoc.unesco.org/go.php, January 2014.

United Nations Educational, Scientific and Cultural Organisation (UNESCO). (2012). *UN system task team on the post-2015 UN development agenda. Education and skills for sustainable development beyond 2015.* Thematic think piece. Retrieved from http://www.unesco.org/new/fileadmin/MULTIMEDIA/HQ/post2015/pdf/Think_Piece_Education.pdf, March 2014.

chapter 4

A CLIMATE FOR CHANGE?
VERTICAL AND HORIZONTAL COLLEGIAL RELATIONS IN TVET COLLEGES

Volker Wedekind and Zanele Buthelezi
Centre for Research in Education and Labour (REAL),
University of the Witwatersrand

Introduction

There is little argument that technical and vocational education and training (TVET) colleges have increasingly moved to centre stage of education and development agendas in South Africa. Where the first two decades of democratic South Africa's education debate focused on the schooling system and, to a lesser extent, the university system, current policy and public discourse sees the post-school system and particularly the TVET colleges as central to addressing a range of social issues, including skills shortages, skills gaps, and youth unemployment. While the institutional setting, the resources, the curriculum, and the governance structures have all been researched, there has been very little focus on the lecturers in the institutions. Where there has been some attention on lecturers, it has tended to focus on their qualifications (or lack thereof) or their work experience. What is not discussed are the daily interactions that make up the quotidian of life in the colleges, and how this may assist or hinder the development of the post-school system and the colleges in particular. This chapter attempts to add to the literature by focusing on the issue of collegial relations and collegiality in colleges and highlight the complexities of working life that shape the climate within which change occurs.

The chapter draws on biographical interview data collected as part of a larger research project into the lives and careers of TVET teachers. The lecturers who were interviewed were selected because they had more than 10 years' experience in the college system and had experienced many of the key reforms during the period 2000–2010. The particular focus of this chapter is on the collegial relations in colleges and their impact on the work of lecturers. The interviews were not explicitly focused on this issue, but it was a major recurring theme that emerged from the data analysis.

The chapter starts by providing clarification of terms such as 'colleague', 'collegial relations', and 'collegiality'. This is followed by a brief discussion on the conceptual framework and methodology, after which the data from the interviews is presented.

Collegial relations and collegiality

The concept of collegiality in educational organisations has received some attention in the research literature, particularly in schooling and in higher education. The importance of colleagues in the lives and careers of teachers is emphasised both in the literature on school change and in the literature on teachers' lives and careers (Fullan, 1999b; Huberman, 1993; Nias, 1989; Sergiovanni, 2001; Westheimer, 1998). A strong strand of research focuses on the complementarity of collegial relations and professional development, drawing on work by writers such as Senge (1990) and Wenger (2000). The research suggests that positive collegial relations enhance the possibilities for professional development for individuals and groups within schools and contribute to the development of the organisation as a whole (Wedekind, 2001). In one of the very few international studies on collegiality that focuses on TVET institutions, Abebe (2009) confirms this point: TVET schools in Ethiopia 'that facilitate the learning and development of teachers exhibit characteristics of a learning organisation culture where professional collaboration, collegiality and shared leadership are practised' (Abebe, 2009).

A second strand of literature focuses on the role of collegiality in the management and governance of education institutions. Singh, Manser and Mestry (2007) contrast collegial leadership models with technocratic and managerialist models. They argue that complex institutions such as schools (and we would suggest that colleges are equally, if not more, complex) require collaborative and collegial models of leadership rather than technocratic models. They argue that emotional intelligence that supports collegial forms of decision-making 'matters twice as much as cognitive abilities such as IQ or technical expertise' when looking at effective leadership (Singh *et al*, 2007). A similar discussion about collegial governance in relation to higher education can be found in the recent analysis of the transformation of one university in South Africa (Chetty & Merrett, 2014). Chetty and Merrett, citing similar debates at Oxford University, argue that collegial forms of governance, while seemingly inefficient, engender a passionate devotion to the institution and high levels of trust (Chetty & Merrett, 2014: 25). Indeed, their case study demonstrates clearly how technicist and authoritarian forms of management that undermine collegial forms of governance ultimately destroy the social fabric of the educational institution.

Building on these two strands of schooling and higher education literature and applying them to the college sector, this chapter analyses the biographical data from interviews with college lecturers in order to understand the ways in which collegial interactions enhance or inhibit professional development of individuals and the organisation, and the degree to which collegiality has been a feature of the management, governance, and leadership approaches in the college sector.

Conceptual framework

The approach adopted in this chapter is framed by the sociological concept of figurations as developed by the twentieth century sociologist and social theorist, Norbert Elias (Elias, 1924, 1978). Elias argues for a sociology that focuses on processes rather than states or structures and that emphasises relationships between people. These networks of relationships are termed figurations by Elias and constitute all forms of social interaction.

Much of the earlier literature on organisations reified the formal institutional level and lost sight of the instability of institutions and their dependence on the individuals that constitute an organisation or institution. To be sure, there are sets of rules and resources that are relatively stable within an institution, and thus there is an appearance of solidity and autonomy from the individuals who constitute the organisation. However, anyone who has visited educational institutions will know that firstly, they differ from each other as much as there are similarities, and secondly, that institutions change over time, at varying degrees of rapidity and for a range of reasons, including the direct influence or absence of particular individuals within a school.

More recently, 'school culture' is a concept that has been developed to explain processes within schools, although ironically it has itself become first objectified and then anthropomorphised (Fullan, 1999a; Little & McLaughlin, 1993; Nias, 1989; Van Maanen & Barley, 1983). The result is that the concept of school culture is often reified in a way that removes the complex and often unpredictable relations between the individuals – past and present – that constitute school culture (Bascia & Hargreaves, 2000).

A colleague is defined for purposes of this chapter as someone who is connected to a person via a relationship centred on work. Usually the relationship is bounded by a particular school, college or university, but may also apply across institutions when educators interact at that level. At its extreme, all educators in a specific education system may be regarded minimally as colleagues in that the myriad relationships between them constitute the figuration often referred to as 'the profession'. Collegial relations in this chapter mean a 'range and intensity of relations that exist between colleagues' (Wedekind, 2001: 150). These relations between colleagues are constantly changing over time as balances of power shift, and need to be viewed as processes that are simultaneously generative and restrictive.

One of the possible outcomes of collegial relations, through the generation of resources and capital of various types, is an experience of collegiality, by which we mean a sense of common identity, fellowship, or moral climate amongst the people interrelating. Ideally, the most important features of collegiality include cooperation with other colleagues, civil and noble treatment of fellow lecturers, loyalty to the campus and college, and enhancement of an environment in which authority is shared. Collegiality is taken to be a valued end result of collegial relations and has a connotation of respect for one another as colleagues. Collegiality 'carries with it a value attribute' (Wedekind, 2001: 150) and is generally regarded as beneficial (Sergiovanni, 2001). One of the issues that we examine in this chapter is the processes through which collegial relations generate collegiality.

Methodology

The data on which the chapter is based is drawn from a larger project on TVET college lecturers in South Africa.[20] The larger project was focused on deepening our understanding of lecturers' knowledge, experience, and practices in the context of a rapidly changing system.[21] The project comprised a number of sub-projects, including three that focused on life histories of various lecturers in the system. In total, 20 lecturers at five different colleges were interviewed between 2010 and 2012 using a focused life history approach, a methodology adapted from earlier work by the author (Wedekind, 2001). The interviews lasted between 45 minutes and an hour each, and each lecturer was interviewed two or three times. Interviews were transcribed and then coded on the basis of emerging themes. These themes form the basis of the analysis that follows.

Context

There is a growing body of literature that has documented the significant changes that have affected colleges since 1994 (Akoojee, 2008; Kraak & Hall, 1999; McGrath & Akoojee, 2007; Powell, 2012; Wedekind, 2010). While we cannot rehearse this in detail here, it is no exaggeration to suggest that TVET colleges have seen some of the most far-reaching and sustained reforms of any part of the education system. While the colleges have

---

20 This research was supported through a research partnership with the South African Qualifications Authority (SAQA) and the University of KwaZulu-Natal. This support is gratefully acknowledged. The findings, opinions, and recommendations of the researchers do not reflect the official SAQA position.

21 See: Wedekind *et al* (forthcoming).

remained largely out of the general public eye, they have been a focus for policy-makers and officials who have introduced changes at all levels. These have included the total transformation of the institutional landscape through mergers of about 150 colleges into 50 mega-colleges, as well as changing the curriculum and the type of students being recruited, introducing new funding formulae, changing management and governance structures, shifting the employer from provincial departments of education to college councils (and now back to the national Department of Higher Education and Training [DHET]), introducing new qualification requirements for lecturers, and running various small and large scale programmes through the colleges. There has been significant turnover of college staff over this period as older lecturers have retired, opted to remain with the provincial departments to avoid changes in their conditions of service, or secured more lucrative employment elsewhere. This staff turnover has resulted in quite significant changes in both the demographics of college lecturers and the typical trajectory that lecturers have followed to get into the colleges. Whereas historically many lecturers would have entered a college after experience in the workplace, many new lecturers are being recruited directly from their place of study without work experience.

The analysis of the data from the interviews provides an insight into how collegial relations (both horizontal and vertical) have been affected and shaped by the context described above. The remainder of this chapter examines the patterns that emerge and how figurations alter as a consequence of these relations.

Colleagues and collegial relations

The first section looks at horizontal collegial relations amongst colleagues within a campus. The discussion, which is illustrated with extracts from the interviews conducted with college lecturers, focuses on generational dynamics, race and racism, and disciplinary specialisations as three categories around which collegial relations are shaped.

Generational diversity amongst colleagues

A generation is a group of people defined by age boundaries and who were born during a certain era and shared similar experiences and social dynamics when growing up (Pilcher, 1994). In the context of this chapter, two cohorts of TVET college lecturers, namely, those who have worked in TVET colleges for more than 10 years and those who have fewer than 10 years of work experience in a TVET college, constitute different generations. Each of these cohorts appears to have its own distinct values, attitudes, habits, behaviours and needs determined by the lecturers' experiences in their lives and work. These experiences have shaped the identity of these individuals, differentiating them from their colleagues in the college environment, and the differences between older and younger lecturers surfaced during the interviews. Besides the generational gap, differences due to gender, race and ethnicity were also touched on.

The interviews revealed that older staff members perceive that their younger colleagues see them as dictatorial, conservative, dogmatic, and rigid in their thoughts and actions (Levin, 2001). While older staff members perceive some younger staff members to be respectful of others, well behaved, hardworking and willing to share their expertise and listen to other peoples' ideas, the majority of younger staff members are seen in a negative light. Here follows an excerpt from an interview with an older member of staff:

> Lately, the majority of lecturing staff in this campus is very young. I began to notice this when the NCV started.[22] There are about five of us who are between 40–53 years old. The majority are young men and women below 35 years, some of whom have been in the college prior to the NCV. The age difference is sometimes a big problem. There are things we do and younger staff members think we are being conservative. Likewise, their way of doing things sometimes seem very immature to older staff like me.

This intergenerational diversity leads to differences of opinion and differences in values, ideas, and choices that may affect work dynamics and lead to misunderstandings and conflict.

Older interviewees also mentioned that some of the younger staff members have modern views and perceive their older colleagues as having obsolete ideas and not being open to change and new concepts. This tends to confirm that older staff members become 'ardent complainers' (Huberman, 1993: 10), in line with Huberman's notion of conservatism. (Huberman 1993). Levin (2001) argues that older staff members are often more discreet, shrewd, sceptical of reform, and less tolerant of younger staff members. Older lecturers feel that they are wiser because of the experience that they have accumulated over the years.

An older interviewee felt that some of the younger lecturers mingle too casually with students and as a result find it difficult to discipline students who are out of line. As lecturers, they are professionally and bureaucratically accountable and need to uphold educationally meaningful standards. The interviewee further suggested that while the experience of older staff members should be seen as an asset to the college community, their ideas are sometimes side-lined in meetings, and more so when lecturers are required to work in teams.

All except one lecturer interviewed for this study affirmed having had experiences of intergenerational misunderstandings with colleagues. Lecturers agreed, nonetheless, that working together at a horizontal, peer, and collegial level is important, especially to allow the cross-pollination of ideas in meetings and when working as teams. The responses of interviewees point to the need for better generational understanding to enhance the working environments of lecturers and improve collegial relations for the benefit of college communities.

---

22 The National Certificate Vocational (NCV) is a qualification introduced in 2008. The NCV is a full-time, three-year programme that is equivalent to Grades 10–12 in the schooling system, and its introduction signalled a shift in the function of colleges to delivering a more school-like curriculum to younger students.

Race relations

A number of interviewees described traces of hostility that sometimes exist between colleagues due to racial tensions linked to the apartheid past. Mergers of colleges rearranged and reshuffled lecturing staff, bringing together people with 'diverse socio-genetic differences' (Wedekind, 2001: 268). The intermeshing of staff of different races has not been easy for lecturers – when people work together, emotions are involved. Kelchtermans (2005) argues that 'emotions are understood as experiences that result from teachers' embeddedness in and interactions with their professional environment' (Kelchtermans, 2005: 997). Furthermore, Nias (1996) argues that a teacher cannot be 'disengaged from his or her cultural, social and historical contexts' (Nias, 1996).

The majority of the lecturers interviewed affirmed that they had, in one way or another, been affected by the social divisions created by apartheid:

I started teaching at campus [XX]. I was the second black lecturer on campus. I can show you a picture. Here, this was us. This was in 1997. Being a black staff member at a predominantly white campus was hard. Uyazi ke isitulo siyashisa uma umnyama phakathi kwezinye izinhlanga ... [You know that the seat is hot when you are black amongst people of other races ...]

The expression 'that the seat is hot' indicates that things are uncomfortable for a black person in a predominantly white environment, and the response seems to suggest feelings of exclusion, discrimination, and alienation of people based on race. This mirrors societal divisions that still exist in reality and in peoples' minds, even in the post-apartheid era. Such a situation is unlikely to lead to positive collegial relations unless it is addressed by concerned college staff and management.

A second interviewee confirmed this state of affairs, asserting that while apartheid may have been destroyed constitutionally, it still exists in some lecturers' minds and manifests itself in their behaviour:

If you get into our staff room you will find the majority of lecturers seated according to race. I mean people of the same race usually sit together. I don't think people do it consciously, it just happens like a habit. There could be many reasons why it occurs. One of them may be is that our historical backgrounds still affect us a lot; separate development still lives in our minds I think. So far it's not easy to get rid of it in our generation. May be our children and grandchildren will be able to but it's difficult for us. Sometimes it's more about being comfortable because you will speak your own language. But sometimes it's because there are people you don't trust who will use anything they know against you.

In addition to reflecting the consequences of apartheid's separate development ideology, the response also reveals group-building push and pull factors in relation to distrust, tension, and fear of backstabbing.

Over and above race, another lecturer argued that being female as well as black aggravated the already strained collegial relations:

My first job was at [XX] Technical College in 1997. I had not planned to be a teacher but that was the only job I could find at the time. This was a white technical college and I was the second black female to be hired in that institution. We were the only blacks there. Challenges of being a black female member of staff in a white institution were enormous. Although a few colleagues were very accepting, the majority were very cold towards us. In meetings we, black females, were close to being invisible. I am not a shy person and am very assertive but I ended up feeling that my opinion did not matter. You would always find the two of us sitting together and there was always that feeling of being treated like a stepchild.

The responses quoted above affirm the existence of in-group advantage and out-group disadvantage among college lecturers. In-group advantage refers to a situation in which members of a group perceive themselves as better than and superior to members of another group. The other group then becomes the out-group and is at a disadvantage, especially if its members are in the minority. In the above instance, the black female college lecturers perceived their white colleagues as a group that consciously or unconsciously alienated them. The black female lecturers were themselves drawn to each other due to their being new and to their shared skin colour, language, culture, and gender.

The black female lecturer further expressed feelings of 'not being seen' or not being acknowledged by her colleagues during meeting interactions. The tone in her response suggests that she believes her contributions and opinions are not valued by colleagues. However, she perceives her abilities differently and does not accept being belittled. A sense of alienation is evident, as she chooses not to contribute and even sits alone in the staff room. This severely limits her social interaction in the work environment and demonstrates unhealthy collegial relations.

Another interviewee spoke about the way intergenerational diversity is influenced by racial inequities and injustices of the past: older staff members come largely from one racial group and cultural background, while new staff are much more diverse. This interviewee added that some of the lecturing staff at the college are foreign nationals:

In our campus it is not bad but in others like campus [XX] which is close to Swaziland and Mozambican borders xenophobic misunderstandings and conflicts amongst staff occur quite often ...

As xenophobic attacks have been prevalent in South Africa in recent years, TVET college lecturers are not disconnected from these dynamics, and college campuses need to be understood as smaller units of a bigger global picture.

Some lecturers revealed feelings of distrust and suspicions that they were being set up for failure and attributed this to racial differences. Some lecturers asserted that they feel under pressure to prove to their colleagues that they possess the required pedagogical and content knowledge, and resented insinuations that they may not be knowledgeable enough or may be inadequately equipped to execute their teaching roles as lecturers:

The subject I had come to teach had a high failure rate. This is the main subject that was allocated to me to teach. There was no induction and mentoring. Things were very hard at first. I felt like I was thrown at the deep end to either swim or sink. I felt like management and senior colleagues in the college wanted me to either fail or prove that I could do it. I did everything I could, including extra classes, to see to it that I did not fail. I think a combination of hard work, luck and God being on my side helped me to pull through. Results for the subject slightly improved that semester. But I can tell you that it is very hard to work in an environment where one has to prove herself all the time.

Although most of the lecturers' responses to questions regarding race were negative, one interviewee indicated that relations improved over time as lecturers got to know one another. This demonstrates the positive effect of familiarity. The interviewee explained that during the first few years of the merger, collegial relations were severely constrained, but difficulties were gradually minimised due to continual peer interaction. Diversity is seen by this interviewee as presenting opportunities to learn more about other people, even from negative experiences. This lecturer emphasised the need to turn negative experiences into learning experiences from which to grow and sees spending time on negative reflection as a futile exercise that affects healthy collegial relations. The interviewee criticised chronic negativity:

Diversity is quite interesting because you learn a lot from it even if negative things come up. Challenges with regards to relations as colleagues have always been there and some have been very bad incidents. I have taught myself to learn something even if it's a bad incident at work. Like harsh criticism, why not look at it closely and see if there isn't a lesson or two from it? I am not saying it never hurts but negativity is stressful and I always want to come out of it a better person.

The interviewee further stated that people may be quoted out of context and incidents blown out of proportion and wrongfully labelled as racist, which does not contribute towards building healthy collegial relations:

But I think there are times when I might have misread or misinterpreted what was happening or what was said. For example, this group of older female colleagues who are senior lecturers and are perceived to be claiming being better than and looking down upon others. I used to believe this although I had never witnessed or had a direct negative encounter with them as alleged. But I have worked with them for many years now and I am beginning to think that there are other issues other than race. Surely what brings them together is a combination of things like age, gender, seniority and also race. I am neither condoning their acts nor perceiving them as saints but I am saying there might be other factors at play …

Interestingly, some responses suggest that colleagues from a particular campus see themselves as a cohesive group in relation to other campuses, and in these instances racism seemed to fade. The shift from singular to plural words like 'we', 'us' indicates a sense of belonging and loyalty to their particular campus and illustrates Elias's (1978) views on the use of pronouns. Elias argues that one's sense of personal identity is closely connected with the 'we' and 'they' relationships of one's group, and with one's position within those units of which one speaks as 'we' and 'they' (Elias, 1978: 128):

> We at campus [XX] and [XX] are not fairly treated. You would swear we are satellite centres or stepchildren ...

> Lecturers from other campuses are more privileged than us. They get everything they ask for in terms of resources. I think we are not treated equally ...

All lecturers are woven into the network of people on their specific campus, regardless of the other divisions that exist between these individuals. A spatial dynamic thus also interweaves identity in so far as common issues on a campus may provide the basis of a common identity.

Being accepted, recognised and liked by one's colleagues matters:

> One incident I will never forget was when I got married in August. More than half the colleagues, of all races mind you, even management, came to my wedding. I thought I was dreaming when I saw them at my wedding! It was such a good feeling. It made me realise that I am one of them!

This is the same lecturer who described how she 'earned respect of and acceptance by colleagues' when results for her subject which had had a very high failure rate improved. The lecturer was gradually establishing more reference groups (Nias, 1989) to identify with, a crucial aspect for one's survival and for the creation of a better work environment. The lecturer went on to explain that these were critical incidents in her work life that made her reconsider her way of thinking and caused her to change her attitude towards others and establish a new sense of self (Huberman, 1992; Schempp, Sparkes & Templin, 1999; Sparkes, 1994).

Specialisations

TVET colleges offer approximately 18 National Certificate Vocational (NCV) programmes and a variety of National Accredited Technical Education Diploma (NATED) courses. Different sub-field programmes make provision for a high degree of specialisation, with the major specialisations being Engineering, Business Studies, Information Technology, and Primary Agriculture. Bigger and more isolated campuses may provide all of these under one roof, depending on the demands of the communities the colleges serve. In colleges that have different campuses in close proximity to each other, a campus may be responsible for only one or two major specialisations. We interviewed lecturers from the fields of Engineering, Information Technology, and Agricultural Studies, and this section will therefore focus primarily on issues of collegiality and collegial relations within these academic departments.

Collegial relations amongst people who are specialists in the same field tend to be stronger than relations amongst colleagues in general. Elias (1978) argues that it is possible that people bond to each other due not only to the division of labour or occupational specialisation, but also to a common sense of identity and shared antagonism towards others (Elias, 1978: 175). Sharing a specialisation thus brings people closer together and colleagues form small beneficial communities within their areas of specialisation:

> *But I relate better to people who also teach computer related courses like me. I am talking about people of all races. We are able to rely on one another for support because of what we teach. We discuss things, share ideas and get information from experienced colleagues. Most of them are not selfish at all ...*

Areas of specialisation were found to be good environments for learning through collaborative efforts. Sharing of ideas and information enables personal and professional development.

The issue of the perceived dominance of Mathematics, Engineering and Pure Science subjects over 'other' subjects was communicated in the responses of lecturers who teach the 'other' subjects, such as Primary Agriculture. The dominant subjects are accorded a higher status and regarded as academic disciplines because of their perceived value in intellectual fields and their link to economic growth and profit, while the 'other' subjects are regarded as 'soft disciplines' and are looked down on. When interrogated further, lecturers identified Marketing, Management, Hospitality, Cosmetology and Tourism as 'other' subjects. The labelling of different areas of specialisation and identifying lecturers in this manner does not contribute to positive collegial relations; lecturers in the so-called 'stronger' disciplines may be resented by lecturers in the fields considered 'weak':

> *I teach Soil Science and I love it ... but the stigma of being a 'weak science' falls on my subjects too ...*

The perceptions of colleagues about each other's status and what they think and say about each other has an impact on the work environment. An interviewee indicated that teaching in a field that is regarded as second-rate results in feelings of inferiority and discomfort when amongst other lecturers, and may lead to low self-esteem which adversely effects relations with colleagues and performance at work.

Working together in teams for the realisation of departmental and campus goals leads to gains in the form of professional development and empowerment. Interactivity and reciprocity is solidified by the ability of people to work together in a team. In this study, data revealed that knowledge accumulated through experience was shared with new and inexperienced colleagues, although one interviewee felt his experience was not valued by younger members of staff. Collaboration, teamwork, peer coaching, partnerships, mentoring, and professional development were all mentioned as important mechanisms for building collegial relations within academic departments.

Relations with college management

The discussion thus far has focused on what we have termed horizontal collegial relations amongst colleagues at campus and academic department level. Section two turns to a discussion of the vertical collegial relations between lecturers, campus leadership, and top college management based in a central office or college headquarters.

A TVET college may have five or more campuses and is headed by the college principal. Each campus is under the leadership of a campus manager who reports to top college management at the central office.

Our research revealed significant resentment from lecturers directed at central office management and the college councils. College councils are made up of external representatives nominated by the Minister of Higher Education and Training as well as community and local industry representatives. The council is the highest governance structure in a college. At the time of the interviews, college councils were also the employers and there was significant unhappiness with how colleges were being run. Dissatisfaction with government as the originator of policies affecting the lecturing staff in colleges was also expressed. Most of the lecturers interviewed raised systemic and institutional challenges. The thorny issues that have led to bad relations between lecturers, college management, and government revolved around ineffective facility and resource management, management capacity, centralisation of power, and lecturer employment status.

Before these issues are discussed in more detail, we briefly highlight the significance of complex networks of interdependent lecturers and officials and their shifting, asymmetrical power balances. In his game models, Elias (1978) elaborates on how the order of complexity in a social change phenomenon increases as the number of players involved increases. The number of interconnected players in different tiers makes the situation more complex, thus making the change process increasingly unpredictable and beyond the ability of any single individual or group of players to control (Dopson, 2005).

Dictatorship, nepotism and lack of collaborative strategies

The majority of lecturers interviewed in this study demonstrated very low levels of trust in their managers and perceived the managers as ineffective. The lecturers believe that the government hires people whose competencies are questionable. The majority of respondents are of the opinion that members of interview panels hire their friends or relatives. Lecturers seem to be convinced that people who are well qualified may not necessarily be employed if they are not acquainted with management in one way or another. The majority of lecturers believe that limiting the selection of candidates for college posts to acquaintances hinders progress and is a grave error which will have long-term effects:

> *Most people in senior positions in our campuses and central office are not fit to be in those positions. Some of them know nothing about technical and vocational education. How does a school principal who has never worked in technical colleges become a rector in a TVET college? Most of management do not have a clue about what we do here. We always wonder how most of them get the top jobs. Is it through bribery or nepotism? We have capable people within the sector that we believe can do the job but those are rarely selected ... this needs to be addressed otherwise it will take a long time before colleges work effectively ...*

A second interviewee concurred that there is a dearth of competent managers in TVET colleges, but added that senior managers (heads of departments, campus managers, the principal and his or her deputies) are struggling due to lack of capacity and training and the expectations placed on them:

> *I don't think our senior managers have the capacity and ability to handle the changes themselves. They are also under pressure to facilitate change and demonstrate to us that they understand what is happening. I think deep down they are also struggling especially because they too never had adequate training to be able to manage the changes …*

Some of the lecturers think it is unfair of management to demand high quality work when managers themselves have a superficial grasp of the challenges faced in the colleges. An interviewee described being disappointed with the 'aloof' response of a deputy manager alerted to a problem being experienced in a workshop. The deputy manager responded that 'I don't want people who come to me with problems but I prefer those who also provide potential solutions to those problems. Right now I am busy and you are wasting my time'.

> *I was disappointed. I believed that he should have given us a chance for further discussions because we did have suggestions about what could be done about the problem. Dismissing us like that made me feel like a school child in the principal's office. I felt put off and I vowed to never go there again …*

The lecturers expected to be listened to, but the deputy manager's response made them feel unwelcome and that their contribution had no value. Other negative experiences with management relate to lecturers' workloads. For example, some lecturers were not given the opportunity to teach their major subjects or to choose which subject they would teach, but were allocated without consultation to any subject that lacked a teacher at the time.

Elias (1978) draws our attention to the concepts of 'function' and 'power' in a relationship. According to Elias, unevenness of function and power signifies interdependencies which constrain people to a greater or lesser extent. He argues that 'when a person lacks something which another person has the power to withhold, the latter has a function for the former'. He further argues that people who are interdependent are not necessarily equally interdependent (Elias, 1978: 78). Allocation of lecturers to subjects without consultation is an example of a lecturer–management relationship which is uneven and conflict bearing. The scenario illustrates how uneven relationships can damage professional work and the emotional well-being of the people concerned, inhibiting the implementation of reform.

The interviews also revealed a great deal of resentment directed at college management from lecturers who are on the college council payrolls. Interviewees complained that lecturers' salaries are not market-related and payment dates and amounts fluctuate constantly. Interviewees constantly referred to management as 'them', identifying managers as part of a distinct, other group. The physical distance between management and the campuses and the isolation of central offices which are far from campuses aggravates the resentment and results in emotional detachment and disaffection, a situation which does not yield collegial relationships.

It is not only senior managers who are resented and seen as not doing their jobs properly and timeously; managers in the human resource units of campuses, central offices, and government offices are also the subject of lecturers' disaffection:

> *HR at our campus is of no help. We only go there to pick up our pay slips and you are lucky if you found an administrator who will be willing to give you help. The central office is worse, you won't find help there. I know for sure they wouldn't have helped me especially because I am still under government payroll. If your employment has not been transferred to Council yet, it's better to bypass them and deal with government directly ...*

The use of negative phrases such as 'these government offices', 'HR is of no help', 'the central office is worse' 'you won't find help there', and 'bypass them' is indicative of a lack of trust, teamwork, and support. In any educational institution, administrators, managers, and professional staff need to work collaboratively to ensure proper coordination and execution of the institution's day-to-day activities and long-term plans. Constrained relations between staff members at different levels adversely impact the effective and smooth running of an institution.

Generational and race dynamics which, as discussed earlier in this chapter, affect horizontal working relationships in the colleges may affect vertical collegial relationships in the same way. For example, an interviewee asserted that intergenerational misunderstandings may occur and may be aggravated by cultural and gender differences, as well as the unique South African historical experience of racial segregation. This lecturer also feels that people have to be conscientised about these differences because they influence people's attitudes and could make or break collegial relations:

> *Take our campus management, for example, they are older, White, Afrikaans speaking females. They may be influenced by culture, historical background, age, and gender. This doesn't necessarily have to cause problems when handled well by both management and staff. But it isn't, as the dividing line becomes too thick and most people see them as very alienating and this is bad because they are in management and should be getting along well with staff. Unless people are made aware of these factors, misunderstandings are bound to occur. This definitely does impact organisational relationships or the working environment positively. Management should lead by example in sorting these things out.*

Colleagues and senior staff members who are in management positions should be proactive in sorting out disparities that arise from differences in culture, gender, history and race.

Centralisation and decentralisation of power

This study also highlighted tensions and contradictions resulting from centralisation and decentralisation of authority in the educational reform processes. Rogers (2010) argues that in centralised approaches, the overall decisions of reform are controlled by the state, as opposed to decentralised approaches that are client-controlled with wide sharing of power and control among stakeholders (Rogers, 2010). In South Africa, key decisions regarding the TVET colleges rested with national and provincial governments without much participation at institutional level. Interviewees feel that this authoritarian attitude supported by an oversized bureaucracy results in the stagnation of change processes and the alienation of lecturers as professionals and critical role-players in the diffusion of innovations. The reform process is perceived to be a closed box that excludes and silences professional input from the majority of lecturers.

Although TVET college lecturers understand the advantages of centralising authority, such as ensuring accountability, they feel that the management of colleges is over-centralised; even trivial issues that could be handled at a campus level are required to be dealt with by the central offices:

> *Even if you want seeds for our gardens, you have to send paperwork for a request to the central office that is 200 km away from campus. Things take a very long time to be processed. Bear in mind that planting is seasonal, by the time the money to buy seeds comes the season for that vegetable is already over. Imagine! Out of season! When you question things you are reminded of the famous motto: 'We have to follow protocol'!*

This lecturer's statement indicates the extent of the bureaucracy and unnecessary red tape and illustrates the type of decisions that could be devolved to campuses. Since campuses are the sites of activities, campus staff are better able to attend to some issues than the staff at the central offices. Further, an interviewee described how major decisions that 'come from above', that is, are taken at central-office level, do not always match the context in which they are intended to be implemented:

> *At one stage a top-down decision for production of grass at our agricultural campus failed. Management had to ask for our comments. The project wouldn't have survived in that climate. We know the area and its demands better. I think no viability study was done before directing this project to our campus. We lecturers have better ideas about what could work this side of the country. When things fail it is bad for us in the eyes of community. We have to explain and it is hard. It is funny how we are never asked about what we think and be given a chance of being professionals.*

The interviewee was made to feel insignificant and disheartened by top-down decisions from the central office, and feels that lecturers should be allowed to give input as they are closer to the 'customer' (Moyo, 2007). In this context, customers are students and local communities whose needs the campuses are meant to respond to. Not being given discretion at campus level, and being dictated to by central office, leads to resentment towards management and the lack of a 'collaborative educational environment' (Singh *et al*, 2007: 542). The interviewee's tone suggests a breakdown in collegial relations between the campus and central office. Further, central management's lack of understanding of local conditions led to the failure of the project which damaged the community's trust in the college.

The lecturers' comments as a whole seem to be a call for more flexibility and collaborative decision-making, especially in matters concerning the community. Veugelers and Zijlstra (2002) argue for collaboration and participatory leadership as strategies that promote collegiality because they are attempts to balance top-down and bottom-up approaches. Such strategies could contribute to a collegial environment in which staff, parents, management, and other stakeholders participate to take the TVET colleges forward. A mismatch between community needs and what the college campus provides puts campus management and lecturers in a difficult situation, as the TVET colleges have to account to the communities with which they work. The need for college and campus managers and lecturers always to consider the broader figurations consisting of parents and the immediate communities served by the colleges emerged in the interviews as a recurring theme.

Comments of some of the interviewees give rise to the perception that transformation of colleges and furthering the skills development mandate is being undermined by the lack of management and leadership skills, including emotional intelligence. Emotional intelligence, from a management perspective, requires management to understand the positive and negative feelings of staff and share leadership in order to work collaboratively and allow collegiality to flourish (Gardner & Stough, 2002). This calls for intellectually capable leaders who also possess emotional intelligence. Thilo (2004) argues that emotionally intelligent leaders have a better chance of improving relationships with staff, lowering employee turnover, improving collaboration amongst colleagues, experiencing greater job satisfaction, and succeeding in their leadership roles.

There were a few instances mentioned of positive managerial practices that enhance collegiality. Most of the collegial learning and sharing of ideas happens during meetings:

> *We have meetings every Thursday afternoon. We are usually tired at this time of the day but these are important as we share what has happened during the week and plan for the following week. No one wants to be out of the loop, so most of the time everybody attends. The HoD chairs the meetings but sometimes chairing of meetings rotates so that we all get a chance to learn. I gain a lot from these meetings because our HoD allows us to discuss issues and make decisions.*

Many lecturers said that they were motivated by commendations, recognition of achievements, and gestures of affirmation from senior management:

> *At one stage, colleagues referred a new member of staff to me as a mentor in computer teaching. This says a lot in terms of being regarded as good at what you do. I felt good and this made me more confident ...*

Overall, managing mega-colleges with multiple campuses is a task that even experienced, appropriately qualified, vocationally oriented managers are battling with (DHET, 2013; Moyo, 2007; Nzimande, 2010). This section suggests that the harmonisation of centralised and decentralised management approaches is a necessity to improve collegial relations between college management and staff.

Conclusion

In summarising his findings from a study on the professional development of TVET teachers in Ethiopia, Abebe (2009 : 244) encapsulates many of the central issues discussed in this chapter:

> *The results of this research pointed that there is no strong culture of support and collaborations among teachers in the TVET schools. This has limited the potential to learn from one another. Culture of collaboration and support must be established for professional development activities to be successful and bring about changes in beliefs, attitudes and practices in the teachers.*
>
> *Among the factors that help the development of culture of support within the school include developing norms of collegiality, openness and trust, creating and supporting networks, collaboration and coalitions among teachers, and the distribution of the role of leadership among teachers (Lieberman, 1994). Collegiality and collaboration in schools are promoted when there exist openness, trust, respect, ease of communication, and supportive school leadership, among others. (Kurse et al, 1994; Barth 1990; Arnold 2005b)*

Collegiality is thus not simply about being congenial. A collegial environment has a direct bearing on the potential for professional development, lecturer identity formation, and efficient management. Furthermore, collegiality is not only about colleagues relating to and supporting each other, but is also critically about how management interacts with professional staff in the colleges and the degree to which people in colleges identify with each other.

The dominant picture that emerges from the lecturers interviewed for this study is that collegial relations, both horizontal and vertical, are generally poor or problematic. Amongst other issues, lecturers describe traces of hostility between colleagues due to racial tensions of the past, and a tendency to bond better with colleagues of their own racial group. Antagonistic behaviour due to generational diversity and differences in ethnicity, nationality, and gender was also noted.

There is however, some evidence of collegiality. Interviewees asserted that they are drawn towards people who teach in the same subject. Some lecturers spoke about the professional development that occurs through working collaboratively with experienced colleagues. Some management strategies, such as formal and informal meetings in which responsibilities are shared, ideas pooled, and constructive criticism given, are seen as inclusive. Lecturers are also exposed to positive motivating comments, appreciation of effort, commendation and recognition of accomplishments during these meetings.

Too little attention has been focused on the complex figurations that make up a TVET college and how the relations between colleagues can have a material effect on reform and development. Developing management strategies that actively encourage and support the building of collegial bonds between staff members and using more collegial managerial strategies may have positive outcomes, not just in terms of staff morale, but in terms of strengthening the TVET colleges, institutions that are critical to the realisation of so many policy imperatives.

References

Abebe, A. (2009). Influences of individual and contextual factors on improving the professional development of TVET teachers in Ethiopia. Doctoral thesis submitted to the Technische Universität Kaiserslautern.

Akoojee, S. (2008). FET college lecturers: The 'devolving' link in the South African skills development equation. *Journal of Vocational Education and Training*, 60(3): 297–313.

Bascia, N. & Hargreaves, A. (2000). *The sharp edge of educational change: Teaching, leading, and the realities of reform*. London: RoutledgeFalmer.

Chetty, N. & Merrett, C. (2014). *The struggle for the soul of a South African University: The University of KwaZulu-Natal, academic freedom, corporatisation and transformation*. Pietermaritzburg: Self-published.

Department of Higher Education and Training (DHET). (2013). *White paper for post-school education and training: Building an expanded, effective and integrated post-school system*. Pretoria: Department of Higher Education and Training.

Dopson, S. (2005). The diffusion of medical innovations: Can figurational sociology contribute? *Organization Studies*, 26(8): 1125–1144.

Elias, N. (1924). Idee und Individuum: Eine Kritische Untersuchung zum Begriff der Geschichte. Doctoral thesis submitted to the Universität Breslau.

Elias, N. (1978). *What is sociology?* London: Hutchinson.

Fullan, M. (1999a). *Change forces: The sequel*. Philadelphia: Falmer Press.

Fullan, M. (1999b). *What's worth fighting for in your school?* Bristol: Falmer Press.

Gardner, L. & Stough, C. (2002). Examining the relationship between leadership and emotional intelligence in senior level managers. *Leadership & Organization Development Journal*, 23(2): 68–78.

Huberman, M. (1992). Teacher development and instructional mastery. In: Hargreave, M. & Fullan, M. (Eds), *Understanding teacher development*. London: Cassell, pp. 122–142.

Huberman, M. (1993). *The lives of teachers*. London: Continuum.

Kelchtermans, G. (2005). Teachers' emotions in educational reforms: Self-understanding, vulnerable commitment and micropolitical literacy. *Teaching and Teacher Education*, 21(8): 995–1006.

Kraak, A. & Hall, G. (1999). *Transforming further education and training in South Africa: A case study of technical colleges in KwaZulu-Natal. Vol. 1: Qualitative findings and analysis*. Pretoria: Human Sciences Research Council.

Levin, B. (2001). *Reforming education: From origins to outcomes*. London: RoutledgeFalmer.

Little, J.W. & McLaughlin, M.W. (1993). *Teachers' work: Individuals, colleagues, and contexts*. New York: Teachers College Press.

McGrath, S. & Akoojee, S. (2007). Education and skills for development in South Africa: Reflections on the accelerated and shared growth initiative for South Africa. *International Journal of Educational Development*, 27(4): 421–434.

Moyo, N. (2007). The relationship between government policy and management practices at further education and training colleges. Doctoral thesis submitted to the University of Pretoria.

Nias, J. (1989). *Primary teachers talking: A study of teaching as work*. London: Routledge.

Nias, J. (1996). Thinking about feeling: The emotions in teaching. *Cambridge Journal of Education*, 26(3): 293–306.

Nzimande, B. (2010). Minister of DHET spells out vision for FETs. *FET College Newsletter*. Mpumalanga.

Pilcher, J. (1994). Mannheim's sociology of generations: an undervalued legacy. *British Journal of Sociology*, 45(3): 481–495.

Powell, L. (2012). Reimagining the purpose of VET – Expanding the capability to aspire in South African further education and training students. *International Journal of Educational Development*, 32(5): 643–653.

Rogers, E.M. (2010). *Diffusion of innovations*. New York: Simon and Schuster.

Schempp, P.G., Sparkes, A.C., & Templin, T.J. (1999). Identity and induction: Establishing the self in the first years of teaching. In: Lipka, R.P. & Brinthaupt, T.M. (Eds), *The role of self in teacher development*. Albany, NY: State University of New York Press, pp. 142–161.

Senge, P. (1990). *The fifth discipline: The art and practice of the learning organisation*. New York: Doubleday.

Sergiovanni, T.J. (2001). *Leadership: What's in it for schools?* London: RoutledgeFalmer.

Singh, P., Manser, P., & Mestry, R. (2007). Importance of emotional intelligence in conceptualizing collegial leadership in education. *South African Journal of Education*, 27(3): 541–563.

Sparkes, A.C. (1994). Life histories and the issue of voice: Reflections on an emerging relationship. *Qualitative Studies in Education*, 7(2): 165–183.

Thilo, J. (2004). *Emotional intelligence and leadership in the ASC*. Alexandria, VA: American Association of Ambulatory Surgery Centers.

Van Maanen, J. & Barley, S. (1983). *Cultural organization: Fragments of a theory*. Presented at Academy of Management Annual Meeting, Dallas, Texas, 1983.

Veugelers, W. & Zijlstra, H. (2002). What goes on in a network? Some Dutch experiences. *International Journal of Leadership in Education*, 5(2): 163–174.

Wedekind, V. (2001). *A figurational analysis of the lives and careers of some South African teachers*. Doctoral thesis submitted to the University of Manchester.

Wedekind, V. (2010). Chaos or coherence? Further education and training college governance in post-apartheid South Africa. *Research in Comparative and International Education*, 5(3): 302–315.

Wedekind, V. with Buthelezi, Z., Mkhize, L., Towani, J. and Watson, A. (forthcoming). South African College Lecturers: Biography, knowledge, pedagogy. Pretoria: *SAQA Bulletin*.

Wenger, E. (2000). Communities of practice and social learning systems. *Organisation*, 7(2): 225–246.

Westheimer, J. (1998). *Among school teachers: Community, autonomy, and ideology in teachers' work*. New York: Teachers College Press.

chapter 5

PREPARING TVET COLLEGE GRADUATES FOR THE WORKPLACE
EMPLOYERS' VIEWS

Joy Papier, Seamus Needham, Nigel Prinsloo and Timothy McBride

Institute for Post-School Studies, University of the Western Cape

Introduction

Recent government policies, for example the White Paper on Post-School Education and Training of 2013, emphasise the need for public technical and vocational education and training (TVET) colleges to strengthen relationships with the workplace in order to improve learners' chances of obtaining both practical training experience and longer-term employment. The Institute for Post-School Studies, through its vocational studies arm, the Further Education and Training Institute (FETI), has, to date, conducted at least three studies concerning transitions of TVET college graduates into employment.

The first study (McGrath, Needham & Wedekind, 2010) theorises the concept of employability of college graduates and provides an important conceptual backdrop for the subsequent two empirical studies discussed. The second study, a research project conducted for the Department of Economic Development and Tourism in the Western Cape (FETI, 2013), investigated the training of artisans for Engineering industries, where qualified artisans were likely to find employment, and what prospective employers' views were on the preparedness of artisans for work. The third study was concerned with identifying employer needs with the intention of linking employers and TVET colleges in order to create pathways for students into employment opportunities. All three studies have yielded data that suggest how employment prospects of college graduates might be improved, particularly through curricular enhancements that make college graduates attractive to employers.

Research and scholarship in relation to the first two studies contributed towards the framing of the third, an applied research study which took the form of a project designed to facilitate employment opportunities for N6 college students. Employers in three fields of college provision were asked for their views on employability of college graduates within their respective sectors and what they require of entry-level employees. Armed with this information, the project developed a 'work readiness programme' which college graduates participated in just prior to their work placements. Students were midway through their placements at the time of writing, but some indicative feedback from employers and students on the work experience was available and we report on this later.

This chapter consolidates the learnings of these three research projects and presents the employer's perspective with reference to expectations regarding the skills of college graduates entering into three areas in which colleges have traditionally offered training programmes, namely the Tourism and Hospitality, the Engineering, and the Wholesale and Retail industries. The chapter begins with a literature review on TVET college training for work and goes on to describe the project in more detail.

Views from the literature

This overview of the literature relating to TVET colleges' preparation of graduates for finding and retaining employment is organised into three sections that relate to each of the three studies mentioned above. The first section deals with theorising employability, the second with the preparation of Engineering artisans, and the third with curriculum enhancement towards improving employability.

What is employability?

In a comparative study of understandings of employability in the South African and United Kingdom (UK) contexts, McGrath et al (2010) critique reductionist notions of employability that focus narrowly on skills required by employers, noting also the personal and economic circumstances that impact on the availability and take-up of employment opportunities. The literature reviewed in the study contributes substantively to widening the debate on what constitutes employability, particularly in the TVET sector. The authors (McGrath et al, 2010: 6) cite Hillage and Pollard's (1988) concept (albeit contested) of employability:

> [E]mployability is understood as an individual's ability to gain initial employment, maintain employment, move between roles within the same organisation, obtain new employment if required and (ideally) secure suitable and sufficiently fulfilling work. (McGrath et al, 2010: 6)

Although much of the argument made in regard to economic factors that inhibit employment is still valid at the present time, it may be argued that the current policy environment offers greater potential for partnerships that enable employment of college graduates. This change has been brought about by the formation of the Department of Higher Education and Training (DHET), within which both education providers and Sector Education and Training Authorities (SETAs) reside, together with the associated skills funding mechanisms. Statements emanating from the office of the Minister have strongly urged employers, SETAs, and colleges to work together to create on-the-job learning spaces for TVET students in order to improve youth employment prospects and thereby contribute to the economic upliftment of communities.

A number of other writers have sought to develop typologies of employability (see Hillage & Pollard, 1998; De Grip, Van Loo & Sanders, 2004; Fugate, Kinicki & Ashforth, 2004). For the purposes of our discussion, we use the model proposed by McQuaid and Lindsay (2005), as the 'factors of employability' they identified resonate with the studies we examine in this chapter. More specifically, the emphasis on personal skills and competencies as factors which influence employability is echoed in the empirical work undertaken by us in this regard. The following 'individual' factors, or elements of 'education for employability', are extracted from McQuaid and Lindsay's (2005: 209–210) table. Limitations in the scope of this chapter prevent us from setting out the full extent of the model, but the skills and attributes listed below are mirrored in the data gathered from employers in our research some years later. McQuaid and Lindsay (2005: 209–2010) mention the following (employability) skills and attributes, inter alia:

- **Basic social skills:** honesty and integrity; basic personal presentation; reliability; willingness to work; understanding of actions and consequences; positive attitude to work; responsibility; self-discipline.
- **Personal competencies:** proactivity; diligence; self-motivation; judgement; initiative; assertiveness; confidence; act autonomously.

- **Basic transferable skills:** prose and document literacy; writing; numeracy; verbal presentation.
- **Key transferable skills:** reasoning; problem solving; basic information and communications technology (ICT) skills; basic interpersonal and communication skills; emotional and aesthetic customer service skills.

In addition, the model refers to formal and job-specific qualifications that are necessary, as well as a range of 'job seeking' skills, all of which were corroborated during our interviews with local employers. The next section looks more closely at conditions that improve employability prospects, particularly for artisans in the Engineering industries.

Preparing artisans for the workplace

In the Engineering industries, artisan training has historically been by way of apprenticeships based on the official National Accredited Technical Education Diploma (NATED) programmes of the Department of Higher Education and Training. Since 2007, with the introduction of the National Certificate Vocational (NCV), attempts have been made to map this new and very different curriculum structure onto the artisan preparation pathway. This has been a protracted and difficult process. We found that Engineering industry employers appear to be more familiar with the traditional artisan development route through the NATED programmes, and their impressions of college training are based largely on their experience of NATED graduates and on personal experience of having come that route themselves.

Our research delved into the comparative literature on good practices in Engineering training, and we now highlight some of the discernible themes and meta-analyses that have been published pertaining to artisan/apprenticeship training in TVET colleges (Field *et al*, 2009; Rauner *et al*, 2012; Steedman, 2012).

Cooperation and partnership

Steedman (2012), in examining lessons learnt and the conditions necessary for the development of apprenticeships, argues that a vital dimension of successful apprenticeships is that there are good partnerships between the workplace, education providers, the state, and other social partners (e.g. trade unions and employer bodies). It is well understood in the literature that this kind of cooperation is a hallmark of the dual system in Germany and Switzerland (Field *et al*, 2009; Hoeckel, Field & Grubb, 2009; Hoeckel & Schwartz, 2010; Pilz, 2007). Rauner *et al* (2012) argue that the successful establishment of a dual TVET system depends on certain prerequisites being fulfilled. One of these requirements is leadership from government, both local and national, in facilitating partnerships which bring together the relevant role-players and promoting the dissemination of information to all the parties involved (Steedman, 2012: 8, 11):

> *For well over a century now, governments in apprenticeship countries such as Austria, Germany and Switzerland have sought to rebalance the potentially*

unequal relationship between employer and apprentice by legislation which gives the apprentice a legal status and the right to acquire general transferable education and skills alongside more firm-specific skills in apprenticeship. Having insisted on this right, government also pays for this component of apprenticeship thereby becoming a major player in the apprenticeship bargain.

and

Apprenticeship is strongest in countries where both employer and employee representative organisations wholeheartedly support and promote apprenticeship and the conditions necessary for its success. Ongoing social dialogue is the necessary prerequisite for this commitment.

Quality training provision

Quality training – on and off the job – is a cornerstone of good apprenticeship systems (Field *et al*, 2009; Rauner *et al*, 2012; Steedman, 2012). Among other key features, apprenticeships need to be geared to produce high-quality, adaptable, and independent apprentices with robust work identities, and the system needs to be cost- and time-efficient. In this regard, vocational teachers, trainers, and assessors should be well trained, and countries should offer trainer certification (Hoeckel *et al*, 2009; Steedman, 2012). Apprenticeship programmes usually require the apprentice to spend part of his/her time learning off the job in a publicly funded vocational college. Other options are to provide the technical and knowledge elements in the workplace using electronic media. In Australia, in addition to publicly funded colleges, private training providers provide off-the-job training for apprentices and are paid from public funds. Field *et al* (2009) argue that quality control must be carefully applied to apprentice training to ensure that the employers involved deliver on their training responsibilities. At the same time, the quality requirements should not be so demanding as to inhibit employer participation.

Curriculum development

A related matter is the availability of strong and current curricula for quality apprenticeships (Field *et al*, 2009). Rauner *et al* (2012) argue that the curriculum should be derived from the professional work tasks the apprentice will be required to perform, should be developmental in nature, and should form the base of the vocational learning processes in both the enterprise and the vocational school.

Allowing employers to lead curriculum development can be important, as employers know what is needed in particular fields. Hoeckel *et al* (2009) found that Swiss employers had a direct influence on every aspect of apprenticeship – from curriculum content to recruitment, qualifications, and assessment. However, according to Field *et al* (2009), employers may underestimate the generic skills needed for mobility. The strength of the German system in ensuring that short-term benefits do not outweigh educational goals could well be emulated.

Continuous versus sequential training and the need to allow for flexibility

Field *et al* (2009) note that the classic dual apprenticeship training approach involves one or two days of schooling in the TVET institution and three or four days of training and working in the company throughout the three or four years of apprenticeship training. Some occupations demand substantial theoretical and practical training before an apprentice is able to do meaningful work. In such situations, it may be that apprentices need to spend long periods (months, or even up to two years) in a TVET institution or in specialised training centres before working in a company. When prior theoretical knowledge has to be acquired over a long period before the apprentice is able to do meaningful work, and the benefits to the company are slower to materialise, it may be useful for prior practical training to take place in TVET institutions. Alternatively, training organised by a group of companies could be more cost-effective. Most effective systems offer firms the flexibility to choose the system best adapted to their needs. Flexibility regarding the duration of the apprenticeship training is important for both employers and apprentices: flexibility helps ensure that apprentices reach their training objectives, and that the costs and benefits of the training to employers will be in balance (Field *et al*, 2009).

Incentivising employers to offer apprenticeships

A key feature of the German and Swiss systems in particular is the high degree of ownership and engagement by employers. Dif *et al* (2012) note that while employers are fundamental to the success of apprenticeship training, they do not always feel their needs are fully understood. Steedman (2012: 6) goes so far as to argue that incentivising employers 'is the most fundamental requirement of a successful apprenticeship system'. Finegold and Wagner (2002) argue that 'it may be difficult to establish an apprenticeship system where one does not already exist, or even to maintain a successful system if the content of the training and the balancing of the costs are not continually updated to ensure they remain attractive to employers' (Finegold & Wagner, 2002: 683).

The incentive for employers to provide apprenticeship places depends on the benefits employers expect to gain and the costs they expect to accrue. Wolter and Ryan (2011) note that employers may be reluctant to offer apprenticeship places if they anticipate a net cost to themselves. On the other hand, as these authors point out, employers can gain both a production benefit (from apprentices doing productive work) and a recruitment benefit (from being able to identify good potential employees). There are two kinds of apprenticeship costs to employers: firstly, apprentice wages; secondly, the resource costs of training (including teaching materials, the time of experienced employees, mistakes by inexperienced apprentices and wasted resources, remuneration of training staff, and administrative costs). The costs of apprenticeships depend on the quality of the training provided, whether special training is provided to supervisors of apprentices, whether supervisors are granted some additional status and remuneration to reflect their role, and so on. Securing trainers who are experienced, knowledgeable, and eager to teach may require companies to invest in wages to make training positions attractive to highly experienced workers (Field *et al*, 2009).

Steedman (2012: 6) argues that for successful apprenticeship training employers need:

- as little bureaucracy as is compatible with good administration;
- good information and ongoing support from a local organisation/college;
- the right set of incentives to balance costs and benefits; and
- young, well-motivated applicants with a good level of general education.

Flexible pathways

Apprenticeship systems should strive to allow for the mobility of apprentices and the opening up of potential career paths. Fuller and Unwin (2007) argue that progression of apprentices is facilitated by access to underpinning knowledge and the workplace curriculum (the mapping of knowledge, skills, and tasks to be learnt). Further, apprenticeships should afford opportunities for participation (providing breadth and depth), teaching, and learning. Resulting qualifications should be fit for purpose, recognised by higher education institutions and professional bodies, and linked to professional qualification pathways. In companies, employees responsible for apprentices' progress should be designated. Lastly, clear post-apprenticeship pathways and career development should be set out.

Integration of education and training

Field *et al* (2009) summarise good-quality workplace training as:

- Providing a strong learning environment for both hard and soft skills;
- Improving the transition from school to work by allowing employers and potential employees to get to know each other;
- Contributing to output; and
- Linking the provision of training to real labour market needs.

They add that it is

> *complemented by other education and training, since some skills are more effectively taught off the job and workplace training may not always be available because of regional economic weaknesses or economic downturns.* (Field et al, 2009: 79)

Conclusion

The foregoing literature review sketches the largely international knowledge base on what enables successful transition by vocational college students into employment. Whilst conditions for good quality training are largely in the context of training that takes place 'on the job', the conditions identified are also instructive for good-quality pre-employment training, and the project we proceed to describe below, aimed at students still in college, incorporated some of these principles.

Views from the ground: An applied research project

Given the learnings gleaned from the comparative literature and from desktop research, we now turn to the third study referred to in this chapter – an applied research project which solicited local employers' views on the training provided by TVET colleges and used this input to enhance current college programmes. The intention of the research was ultimately to enable college graduate transitions into workplaces and to create sustainable pathways into work for college students.[23]

A reference group comprising provincial education department curriculum officials as well as SETA representatives advised on college curricula as well as sector-related issues, while a specialist college working group brought student support services members into a forum to advise on implementation. It was recommended by the reference group that NATED N6 students be targeted as recipients of the project, as these students are required to obtain internships as a compulsory component of their qualification. In addition, the N6 programme was considered a more flexible option for curriculum enhancement in comparison with the tightly structured and relatively crowded NCV programme which leaves little room for curriculum adjustments to be made.

With the assistance of the relevant SETA, 10 employers per industry sector were identified for in-depth interviews which interrogated the potential capacity of each company to employ new college graduates, as well as the criteria, attributes, skills, and knowledge that the company considered necessary for entry-level employment. In the Engineering sector, 11 companies suggested by the Manufacturing, Engineering and Related Services SETA (merSETA), including two automotive companies, seven manufacturing companies, and the electrical department of a municipality, were interviewed. In the Wholesale and Retail sector, four of the companies interviewed were large food/grocery retailers, three were medium-sized fashion retail stores, two were suppliers in building and construction, and one was a media company. In the hospitality sector, 10 organisations were identified, seven of which were hotels and three of which were other industry-related organisations and forums.

Employers in the Engineering sector

Engineering firms interviewed said they require new entrants to have a range of practical, academic, and attitudinal skills in order to be employable, and expect the formal college syllabus to cover the basic academic and practical training needed. Some companies reported using psychometric testing, including assessments of diagnostic skills and motor coordination/dexterity skills, to assess new entrants.

Regarding practical skills, companies were concerned that the NCV does not provide students with sufficient practice, and one large company in particular mentioned that students frequently fail internal tests set by the employer as part of the employment interview. Similar concerns were raised about students who had NATED theoretical qualifications, although it was noted that some of these students had acquired workshop

---

23 This research project was funded by the DG Murray Trust.

hand-tool skills as part of their college training. Engineering firms view students with college training in practical skills as more employable, since this means 'less work for the company to do'. An additional concern is new employees' exposure to health and safety procedures within Engineering workshops, as well as their experience of working in a workshop environment. One of the firms interviewed felt that students should be able to apply at least 30% of their practical skills to working with workplace machinery. Additional concerns related to the current negative economic environment: since companies are forced to adopt leaner, 'just-in-time' manufacturing approaches, they need students who are reasonably 'work ready'.

Relevant Mathematics and Science knowledge is considered to be a prerequisite underpinning an apprentice or trainee's ability to work in the Engineering sector, specifically in relation to reading and understanding Engineering drawings and specifications. While trainees' knowledge of trigonometry and Pythagorian principles is often found to be lacking, companies indicated that they are unwilling to provide training in mathematical and scientific concepts that they feel should be covered by colleges. New employees embarking on an artisan pathway are also expected to have passed Mathematics, Science, and English at Grade 12 level and have an N3 or N4 qualification. In addition, they are expected to have ICT, electronic communication, and administrative skills. A number of Engineering firms stressed the need for employees to be able to invoice accurately and perform basic administrative functions within the firm.

Companies were vocal on the need for broader cross-cutting skills which fall outside the ambit of the formal curriculum, for example the capacity to think logically in order to interpret and develop appropriate solutions and the ability to read, write, and converse in English. Communication skills were also identified as important, particularly the ability to communicate with a team and individually with peers, mentors and clients. In this regard, a number of firms feel that younger employees often do not show sufficient respect to older, more experienced employees. A few Engineering firms reported holding regular diversity workshops to encourage greater communication and respect within their workforces.

In addition, all of the firms mentioned attitudinal skills as a key factor for employability. Potential employees are expected to show a commitment to learning, and not assume that they have sufficient knowledge for the job on entry. One employer challenged college students' attitudes as follows:

> *The attitude of 'I know everything' must cease – we also have the challenge of dealing with students who feel that 'I deserve more money' – many of these students do not want to start at the bottom.*

It was noted by one company that apprenticeships in the Engineering sector remain 'old fashioned', and that issues of 'respect, neatness, presentation and punctuality' are still very important. Honesty was cited as an important ethic, as well as having sufficient humility to admit to making a mistake. An auto manufacturing employer stated that new employees should demonstrate a passion for the work they are involved in, and that the company preferred an employee with obvious passion to a graduate with better qualifications.

Discipline, punctuality and ethics were stressed as desirable attributes by most of the Engineering firms interviewed. A few companies stated that they need to instruct new employees on mobile phone etiquette, cleanliness of the workstation, and being more environmentally aware. A number of employers asked that career guidance be built into college curricula, as they often received applications from graduates who have little idea of or interest in the specific Engineering job applied for.

Overall, the employers interviewed were concerned that cross-cutting and attitudinal skills critical to maintaining a job and being successful in the workplace are seen as less important than academic and practical training. Companies were not aware of students being prepared in these aspects and asked that colleges address this shortcoming.

Placement prospects

Engineering firms interviewed were asked whether they would be willing to participate in a project to place N6-level college graduates. Most companies were cautious about committing to placement, but did not object in principle, being more concerned about paying stipends which they might not have budgeted for or be able to afford.

Furthermore, companies said they could not commit to employing a particular number of students, as the number they could afford to employ depends on the business cycle; companies indicated they would rather commit to internships than promise direct employment. Graduates would need to 'prove themselves' and would have to follow the companies' internship programmes. The placement process is linked to 'filling the gaps' left in companies as people exited the system.

Respondents stated that there needs to be closer relationships between industry and the colleges regarding work placement, and that companies should be involved sooner rather than later in the process. It was suggested that prospective interns be exposed to companies before being placed to gain an understanding of the rigours of the job and be enabled to make an informed decision about accepting a placement.

Employers in the Tourism and Hospitality sector

Hospitality firms, being located within the Services industry, placed significant emphasis on the need for attitudinal skills, although respondents indicated that foundational academic qualifications and specific occupational qualifications are also necessary to access employment in this sector. Companies added that while practical skills are valued, they are not a prerequisite, as skills are taught on the job on an ongoing basis.

Hotels, as well as the in-house Hospitality training providers interviewed, confirmed that a matriculation certificate is generally seen as a minimum qualification for entrance into the Hospitality sector; however, entrance requirements are not rigidly applied across the industry. An in-house training provider for a chain of hotels said students with Grade 10 and Grade 12 qualifications would be accepted, but would be channelled into specific occupations within the sector that may have limited career mobility. Hotels specified a range of qualifications necessary for career progression, most notably diplomas and degrees for management staff. There are also specific requirements for entry into particular fields, such as having a Diploma in Professional Cookery in order to be trained as a chef. The NCV is recognised within the Hospitality industry as a matriculation equivalent, albeit not well known or understood, and NATED courses also carry recognition within this sector. A few hotels noted the need for candidates to speak English fluently and to have excellent communication skills. Although many hotels recruit graduates from hotel schools that offered post-matric qualifications, TVET colleges are also seen as a source of potential employees.

Despite the requirement for formal qualifications, the hospitality industry allows employment and progression without formal qualifications based on years of experience within the industry. Most employees are appointed in entry-level positions and are expected to work their way upwards over a period of years. Employers view lifelong learning as a necessity for progression.

Additional skills identified as desirable are knowledge of ICT programs that are specific to the Hospitality industry, as well as of standard computer packages such as MS Office. Students are also required to have a general basic understanding of business processes and principles such as budgeting and management systems.

Employers place great value on attitudinal skills, as can be seen from the following comments:

- 'Give me someone with the right attitude – the rest I can teach.'
- 'Attitude is critical in this industry.'
- 'We employ personalities, the skill can be trained.'
- 'A skill can be taught, attitude cannot.'

A number of hotels noted that students, particularly those from TVET colleges, appear to lack job-seeking skills. For example, students' CVs are often of poor quality; students present themselves inappropriately; and students are unable to demonstrate their knowledge of or passion for the industry during interviews. Regarding career guidance, some students appear to be misinformed about the nature of work in the Hospitality industry, which involves long hours and shift work.

Hotels stressed the need for students to see job placement as an expanded job interview, as illustrated in the following comment:

> *If students stay and work for six months, they are more employable as the hotel gets a better sense of them by working with them.*

According to some hoteliers, some students appear not to take practical placements seriously, and this has a serious impact on the hotel and its staff. Nonchalant attitudes on the part of the students, it was said, create a negative impression of the college and jeopardise future placement prospects. A respondent cited examples of student absenteeism and latecoming, which resulted in two people having to do the job of three. She feels that students need a sense of responsibility towards and ownership of their training to the extent that they adjust their lifestyles according to the priorities of the job.

Numerous references were made to the need for students to behave professionally in the workplace, including adhering to a dress code and behaving appropriately in front of guests. One employer noted that increasingly hotel guests look for a positive experience at a hotel over and above 'mod cons and facilities'. Mobile phone etiquette was also cited by hotel employers as a critical behaviour to be addressed in training.

Hotel employers noted that students entering the industry need to be flexible in terms of time frames as well as towards job rotation. Students have to be prepared to start at entry level and maintain a positive attitude while experiencing all aspects of this industry. Concerns were raised that some students feel that certain jobs are 'beneath them' and do not have a strong customer service ethic.

The ability to take initiative and to follow through on instructions are seen as key attributes of 'working independently' by a number of hotel spokespersons, who said that these qualities would increase a candidate's employability and the chances of promotion. In addition, new entrants should be 'people-centred, motivated, and have a vibrant personality'.

Ultimately respondents stressed that what they are looking for in a recruit is the 'right attitude'; the rest, they said, they could teach.

Placement prospects

Respondents in the Hospitality industry noted that the availability of placements is dependent on the market cycle and that timing is important since the industry is seasonal – winter being a 'slow' season and summer the peak season during which demand increases. While unable to commit to providing a fixed number of placements, respondents said graduates have to prove their worth, and selections would be made according to set criteria. Suitable candidates would have to follow in-house internship programmes.

When asked what would enhance the work readiness of college students, respondents stated students should have the right attitude and understand the rigours of Hospitality work. Many graduates expect to start in a management position, whereas they should understand that promotion is on the basis of hard work, innovation, and demonstrated willingness, and that in the hotel industry it takes about 10 years to reap the rewards of promotion.

Employers in the Wholesale and Retail sector

The Wholesale and Retail industry is a wide-ranging domain which comprises a vast range of work contexts, from fashion and grocery stores to call centres, pharmacies, bookshops and so on. Accordingly, qualifications for employment in the Wholesale and Retail sector span a number of skills areas and are classified according to the Organising Framework for Occupations (OFO) codes, for example, NQF Level 2 (Grade 10) qualifications for meat cutters, NQF Level 3 qualifications for bakers, and postgraduate qualifications for trainee managers. Large Wholesale and Retail employers generally require entry-level employees to have a matriculation certificate or an equivalent qualification. Unit standards based qualifications provided in a learnership model are widely used within this sector.

A leading retail employer noted, similarly to the Engineering sector respondent cited previously, that most jobs in this sector require a minimum of a Grade 12 certificate with a 50% pass in the company's English proficiency test. Many employers in this sector offer their own-in-house training programmes, one of which progresses to a Master of Business Administration (MBA) programme. While retail qualifications are not widely offered at public TVET colleges, universities of technology offer programmes resulting in high employment rates for their graduates. An industry trainer noted that TVET college students with a Business Administration qualification struggle in the Wholesale and Retail sector as this qualification does not offer any specific retail focus. Additionally, employers require new entrants to have ICT skills and be proficient in the use of computers.

A sound understanding of English is seen as an important competence for this industry, while practical experience is a key factor affecting employability. Being in the services sector, employers in this industry also place strong emphasis on attitudinal skills. Desirable attributes mentioned include, inter alia, 'professionalism', 'good communications', 'interaction with customers', 'solutions focused', 'time management', 'conflict management', and 'problem solving skills'. Self-discipline and self-management are also viewed as important personal qualities.

At least two companies mentioned that prospective employees should show evidence of casual work experience in the retail sector, and suggested that retailers could cooperate with colleges by offering students company specific training during vacations. A fashion retailer suggested that simulated exercises – for example 'mock' presentations and interactions to demonstrate how employees should conduct themselves – are useful in job preparation for the sector.

Placement prospects

Wholesale and Retail companies indicated that they are willing to place students, but want to be actively involved in the selection process. One respondent noted that at the time of the interview the company had about 20 vacancies and usually employed five to 10 new entrants per year as trainee managers. Respondents from larger retail companies indicated that a store which employs four managers would employ between 50 and 100 staff members, and that each new store opened creates around 100 jobs.

Large retailers who operate call centres are able to offer a relatively large number of positions per year, although graduates might not have envisaged working in a call centre.

It was recommended that companies should be part of the selection process to avoid potential problems arising, and that partnerships in this process are critical. A large fashion retailer said that they employ mostly the local university of technology students because these students had undergone a cooperative learning programme and are therefore 'work ready'. The respondent suggested that colleges adopt a similar programme and mentioned examples of work readiness programmes in other contexts for comparative purposes.

Conclusions from the data

The data collected provides critical insights into the perceptions and requirements of employers in three areas of industry as to what constitutes employability in their respective sectors.

Generally, respondents acknowledged that students are being taught the technical skills in their college courses and largely possess sufficient basic knowledge and skills together with some practical training. Employers feel that some form of 'work preparation' is essential to cover the 'softer' skills not overtly taught and/or practised, and that graduates, in spite of their technical training, have to be 'schooled' in knowledge and understanding of the workplace. Employers do expect, however, a host of 'attitudinal' and other generic skills to be in place.

Skills and attributes

An analysis of the data produced an extensive list of skills and attributes required by employers, and the frequency with which each skill or attribute was mentioned was tallied in order to discern trends and themes. The list is presented below.

- Basic theoretical and practical knowledge;
- Communication skills;
- Computer skills;
- Customer service skills;
- Ability to take initiative;
- An 'ethic' of hard work;
- Self-management skills;
- Willingness to learn;
- Being presentable or well groomed;
- Telephone (mobile phone) etiquette;
- A positive attitude;
- Professionalism;
- Interviewing skills;
- Punctuality;
- Resilience to cope with long hours;
- Respectfulness;
- Teamwork skills;
- Truthfulness/ethics;
- Accountability/taking responsibility; and
- Discipline.

N6 college curricula and cross-cutting/attitudinal skills

The N6 courses in the Engineering (N6 Engineering Studies), Wholesale and Retail (N6 Business Management, N6 Financial Management, N6 Human Resource Management, and N6 Management Assistant), and Hospitality (N6 Hospitality and Catering Services) industries were examined and discussed by the working group to probe whether the skills and attributes identified by employers as 'necessary' skills are being covered in the college programmes.

Although elements of the necessary skills described by respondents were found to exist across the N4–N6 courses in the NATED syllabus, and lecturers are addressing those skills in various ways, the N6 courses do not specifically focus on those skills, nor are the skills covered in any systematic way during students' preparation for the workplace. College personnel said that while some skills might be addressed at levels below N6, students tend to pay little attention to learning these skills. Core subjects[24] focus on the technical skills required in a particular field. In sum, college experts reported that across colleges the skills identified by employers are dealt with in diverse ways and with varying degrees of emphasis.

College staff in the working group (a smaller group of college staff actually working with the students) agreed with the sentiments expressed by employers – that cross-cutting skills might be better dealt with in a focused, targeted, work-preparation programme that should be delivered just prior to N6 students leaving the colleges to seek practical placements for the completion of their qualifications. This practice would prepare students for the workplace and encourage them to see the preparation programme as relevant and timely.

A work readiness programme for college graduates

The data on what companies require of new entrants were matched with the current N6 curricula to ascertain whether the college programmes equip students with the skills, knowledge and attributes required by the companies. In addition, the project team examined the composition of programmes with a similar emphasis offered by other service providers, as well as 'soft skills' courses offered at the colleges.

The analysis revealed learning 'gaps' in the college curricula, and this information was used as a basis for designing a work readiness programme together with a comprehensive set of supporting materials. The list of required skills and attributes identified by the employers in each of the three sectors was categorised in terms of five thematic areas: Professionalism; Communication; Understanding the Workplace; Values and Ethics; and Application of College Learning to the Workplace. These were incorporated into the 'curriculum enhancement' programme. College graduates need training in:

- Being professional;
- Communication skills;
- Understanding the workplace;
- Values and ethics; and
- Application of college learning to the workplace.

As employers across the three sectors identified similar types of skills, it was agreed that a generic set of materials would be developed and would be contextualised for specific situations. The materials developed for the programme are interactive and activity-based. Reference and working group members were consulted throughout the curriculum development process. Input and feedback from learners was considered during the materials development process, and industry role-players were also invited to comment. Their responses were built into subsequent iterations of the materials. In addition, college facilitators were briefed and given the opportunity to provide feedback on the basis of which further adjustments to the programme were made.

---

24 Core subjects are the four subjects specific to the particular NATED programme and relevant to the occupational area.

The programme was delivered to N6 students at three large colleges during the subsequent recess period.

Programme delivery and work placements

The final curriculum enhancement programme is a short course comprising five modules (based on the five thematic areas identified) to be taken by students just prior to being assigned to workplaces as interns and includes two structured (i.e. planned) visits to industry for purposes of student reflection.

To secure internships, employers are encouraged to participate in the college selection procedures. Students are required to sign learning agreements with their colleges and are monitored for the duration of their work placements by college personnel who conduct workplace visits. A stumbling block that emerged was the issue of the payment of stipends to the interns. Employers had not budgeted for these payments and did not necessarily have funds to cover them. SETA representatives encouraged employers to access PIVOTAL[25] grants, but in view of possible administrative delays, it was decided to make project funds available to enable students to take up their internships. This financial support proved invaluable in enabling the project to roll out according to plan.

Outcomes

A major outcome of the project was the interaction that took place between employers and colleges, assisted by SETAs, and the demonstrated understanding and appreciation of the roles played by each of the parties. At the time of writing, at least 60 N6 students had been in work placements for about six months with various employers. The students were being monitored and mentored by college personnel. Follow-up data gathered from both students and employers indicate that:

- Employers appreciate the fact their expressed needs were taken seriously by the colleges. Colleges demonstrated this by incorporating the skills perceived to be lacking into a focused work readiness programme that students could undertake prior to placement.
- Employers, when asked about their experience of the students placed, reported that they were pleasantly surprised by the awareness displayed by students with regard to, inter alia, time on task, punctuality, and a generally positive attitude.
- Students valued the targeted work readiness skills they were exposed to, and mentioned particularly the role-plays during the programme that gave them advance insight into what they might expect on the job. They also valued introductory visits to the companies which meant that students did not arrive 'cold' on their first day of placement.

---

25 The PIVOTAL grant refers to the 80% of SETA discretionary funds that should be directed at PIVOTAL (Professional, Vocational, Technical and Academic Learning) programmes.

While these are relatively early findings, the indications are positive and reassuring and accord well with the literature on employability skills and good training practices. More comprehensive feedback towards the end of the project will be gathered for a final research report that will contribute substantively to our empirical knowledge base on institution-to-work transitions of TVET college graduates.

Conclusion

This chapter has brought together three research initiatives conducted for purposes of understanding and facilitating college-to-work transitions of TVET college graduates. First, the study undertaken by McGrath *et al* (2010) laid an important basis for theorising aspects of employability, especially as cited in the model by McQuaid and Lindsay (2005). Next, the focus on artisan training set out valuable 'good practices' in comparative contexts in respect of the conditions needed for successful training for and in the workplace (on and off the job) that are instructive for pre-employment training as well. Third, the curriculum enhancement of current college training programmes initiated by a donor funded project which focused on facilitating work placements for TVET college graduates was detailed. The applied research project enabled the voices of local employers to be heard, pointing to perceived gaps in college training and suggesting the need for curricula that take account of specific workplace requirements.

Acknowledgement
We extend our grateful thanks to insightful sponsors like the DG Murray Trust who have seen fit to invest in researching this critical phase of education and training for youth and adults in South Africa.

References

Akoojee, S. & McGrath, S. (2005). *Post-basic education and training and poverty education in South Africa: Progress to 2004 and Vision to 2014*. Post-Basic Education and Training working paper series, 2. Edinburgh: Centre of African Studies, University of Edinburgh.

Cloete, N., Needham, S., Net, H., Papier, J., Sheppard, C., & Stumpf, R. (2009). *Responding to the educational needs of post-school youth*. Pretoria: Centre for Higher Education Transformation and the Further Education and Training Institute.

De Grip, A., Van Loo, J., & Sanders, J. (2004). The industry employability index: Taking account of supply and demand characteristics. *International Labour Review*, 143(3): 211–235.

Deissinger, T. & Hellwig, S. (2005). Apprenticeships in Germany: Modernising the dual system. *Education and Training*, 47(4): 312–324.

Deissinger, T. (2001). Vocational training in small firms in Germany: The contribution of the craft sector. *Education and Training*, 43(8/9): 426–436.

Department of Higher Education and Training (DHET). (2013). *White paper for post-school education and training: Building an expanded, effective and integrated post-school system*. Pretoria: DHET.

Dif, M., Sidlauskiene, D., Pranculyte, J., & Spankis, L. (2012). *Funding and stakeholder roles in the development of apprenticeship – What can be learnt from the experience of other countries?*

Presented at the European Conference on Educational Research (ECER): The Need for Educational Research to Champion Freedom, Education and Development for All, University of Cádiz, 2012.

Federal Department of Economic Affairs (FDEA) & Federal Office for Professional Education and Technology (OPET). (2011). *Facts and figures: Vocational and professional education and training in Switzerland.* Bern: Switzerland.

Fersterer, J., Pischke, J.S., & Winter-Ebmer, R. (2008). Returns to apprenticeship training in Austria: Evidence from failed firms. *Scandinavian Journal of Economics,* 110(4): 733–753.

Field, S., Hoeckel, K., Kis, V., & Kuczera, M. (2009). *Learning for jobs: OECD policy review of vocational education and training: Initial report.* Paris: Organisation for Economic Cooperation and Development (OECD).

Finegold, D. & Wagner, K. (2002). Are apprenticeships still relevant in the 21st century? A case study of changing youth training arrangements in German banks. *Industrial & Labor Relations Review,* 55(4): 667–685.

Fugate, M., Kinicki, A., & Ashforth, B. (2004). Employability: A psycho-social construct, its dimensions, and applications. *Journal of Vocational Behaviour,* 65(1): 14–38.

Fuller, A. & Unwin, L. (2007). What counts as good practice in contemporary apprenticeships? Evidence from two contrasting sectors in England. *Education and Training,* 49(6): 447–458.

Fuller, A. & Unwin, L. (2011) The content of apprenticeships. In: Dolphin, T. & Lanning, T. (Eds) *Rethinking apprenticeships.* London: Institute for Public Policy Research, pp. 29–39.

Further Education and Training Institute (FETI). (2013). *Final report: Supply and demand for artisans in the Western Cape – A study conducted for the Department of Economic Development and Tourism.* Wynberg: FETI.

Gamble, J. (2003). *Curriculum responsiveness in FET colleges.* Research Programme on Human Resources Development. Cape Town: Human Sciences Research Council Press.

Glover, R.W., Clopton, L., McCollum, M., & Wang, X. (2007). Building an apprenticeship and training system for maintenance occupations in the American transit industry. *Education and Training,* 49(6): 474–488.

Grollmann, P. & Rauner, F. (2007). Exploring innovative apprenticeship: Quality and costs. *Education and Training,* 49(6): 431–446.

Harris, R., Simons, M., Willis, P., & Carden, P. (2003). Exploring complementarity in on- and off-job training for apprenticeships. *International Journal of Training and Development,* 7(2): 82–92.

Hawkins, T.H. (2008). What is an apprentice? *Education and Training,* 50(1): 24–27.

Hillage, J. & Pollard, E. (1998.) *Employability: developing a framework for policy analysis.* Research Brief 85. London: Department for Education and Employment.

Hoeckel, K. & Schwartz, R. (2010). *Learning for Jobs: OECD Reviews of vocational education and training: Germany.* Paris: OECD Publishing

Hoeckel, K., Field, S., & Norton Grubb, W. (2009). *Learning for Jobs: OECD reviews of vocational education and training.* Paris: OECD Publishing.

Imdorf, C. & Leemann, R.J. (2012). New models of apprenticeship and equal employment opportunity: Do training networks enhance fair hiring practices? *Journal of Vocational Education & Training,* 64(1): 57–74.

International Labour Organization (ILO). (1997). *Human resource development for continued economic growth: The Singapore experience.* Paper presented at the ILO Workshop on Employers'

Organizations in Asia-Pacific in the Twenty-First Century. Turin, Italy. 5–13 May 1997. Geneva: ILO ACT/EMP Publications.

International Labour Organization (ILO). (2010). *Effectiveness, efficiency and impact of Indonesia's apprenticeship programme*. Jakarta: ILO Jakarta Office.

Janse Van Rensburg, D., Visser, M., Wildschut, A., Roodt, J., & Kruss, G. (2012). *A technical report on learnership and apprenticeship population databases in South Africa: Patterns and shifts in skills formation*. Pretoria: Education and Skills Development Programme, Human Sciences Research Council.

Knight, B. & Karmel, T. (2011). Apprenticeships and traineeships in Australia. In: Dolphin, T. & Lanning, T. (Eds), *Rethinking apprenticeships*. London: Institute for Public Policy Research: Association of Colleges, pp. 106–119.

Kraak, A. (2008). Incoherence in the South African labour market for intermediate skills. *Journal of Education and Work*, 21(3): 197–215.

Lange, T. (2012). German training revisited: An appraisal of corporatist governance. *Education and Training*, 54(1): 21–35.

Le Deist, F. & Winterton, J. (2011). *Comparative analysis of apparent good practice in apprenticeship system: Synthesis report on comparative analysis of the development of apprenticeship in Germany, France, the Netherlands and the UK*. Leonardo da Vinci Transfer of Innovations Project, Devapprent: Work package 3b. Luxembourg: European Union.

McGrath, S., Needham, S. & Wedekind, V. (2010). *Reworking employability: Reflections from the English and South African Public Further Education (and Training) college sectors*. Paper presented at the World Congress of Comparative Education Societies 2010, Istanbul.

McQuaid, R.W. & Lindsay, C. (2005). The concept of employability. *Urban Studies*, 42(2): 197–219.

Meyer, T. (2009). Can 'vocationalisation' of education go too far? The case of Switzerland. *European Journal of Vocational Training*, 46(1): 28–40.

Nzimande, B. (2010). Address by Minister of Higher Education and Training, Dr Blade Nzimande, at the Further Education and Training College Summit, Boksburg, 2010.

Perold, H., Cloete, N., & Papier, J. (2012). *Shaping the future of South Africa's youth: Rethinking post-school education and skills training*. Pretoria: African Minds for the Centre for Higher Education Transformation, Southern African Labour and Development Research Unit, and the Further Education and Training Institute.

Pilz, M. (2007). Two countries – system of vocational education? A comparison of the apprenticeship reform in the commercial sector in Switzerland and Germany, *Compare: A Journal of Comparative and International Education*, 37(1): 69–87.

Rauner, F. & Smith, E. (2010). *Rediscovering apprenticeship: Research findings of the International Network on Innovative Apprenticeship (INAP)*. Heidelberg: Springer.

Rauner, F., Heinemann, L., Hauschildt, U., & Piening, D. (2012). *Project report: COMET-Pilot test South Africa including the pilot test Vocational Identity/Occupational Commitment and results of the QRC pilot project*. Prepared as part of the project: Implementing modern VET Research Tools in South Africa: QRC, COMET and VI. Bremen: University of Bremen.

Roodt, J. & Wildschut, A. (2012). Evaluation of the National Skills Development Strategy, 2005–2010. Skills development through structured qualifications: The trade test – a constraint on artisan skilling? *HSRC Review*, 10(1): 24–25.

Schmidt, C. (2010). Vocational education and training (VET) for youths with low levels of qualification in Germany. *Education and Training*, 52(5): 381–390.

Snell, D. & Hart, A. (2007). Vocational training in Australia: is there a link between International Network on Innovative Apprenticeship (INAP) attrition and quality? *Education and Training*, 49(6): 500–512.

Steedman, H. (2010). *The state of apprenticeship in 2010: International comparisons – Australia, Austria, England, France, Germany, Ireland, Sweden, Switzerland. A Report for the Apprenticeship Ambassadors Network*. London: Centre for Economic Performance, London School of Economics and Political Science.

Steedman, H. (2011). Challenges and change: Apprenticeships in German-speaking Europe. In: Dolphin, T. & Lanning, T. (Eds), *Rethinking apprenticeships*. London: Institute for Public Policy Research, pp. 93–105.

Steedman, H. (2012). *Overview of apprenticeship systems and issues – ILO contribution to the G20 Task Force on Employment, International Labour Office, Skills and Employability Department*. Geneva: ILO.

Wildschut, A., Kruss, G., Janse van Rensburg, D., Haupt, G., & Visser, M. (2011). *Learnerships and apprenticeships survey 2010 technical report: Identifying transitions and trajectories through the learnership and apprenticeship systems*. Pretoria: Human Sciences Research Council.

Wolter, S.C. & Ryan, P. (2011). Apprenticeship. In: Hanushek, E.A., Machin, S. & Woessmann, L. (Eds), *Handbook of the economics of education*, Vol. 3. Amsterdam: Elsevier, pp. 521–576.

chapter 6

WHAT WILL IT TAKE TO TURN TVET COLLEGES AROUND? EVALUATION OF A LARGE-SCALE COLLEGE IMPROVEMENT PROGRAMME

Carmel Marock
Independent Research Consultant

Eleanor Hazell
M&E Manager, JET Education Services

Bina Akoobhai
R&D Manager, Swiss–South African Cooperation Initiative

Introduction

The Colleges Improvement Project (CIP) was implemented by JET Education Services (JET) in 15 TVET colleges in the Eastern Cape and Limpopo provinces between September 2011 and December 2014 on behalf of the Department of Higher Education and Training (DHET). The project's overarching strategic objective was:

> To improve the functionality and capacity of the eight Eastern Cape and seven Limpopo FET Colleges, in order to improve teaching and learning and provide the foundations for further learning and improved employability of graduates. (DHET, 2013)

This objective was informed by an initial assessment of the colleges at the end of 2012 which revealed that the colleges were experiencing substantive weaknesses in several functional areas (JET, 2012a and 2012b), and that the colleges were at different levels of functionality. Of the 15 colleges, three were classified as good, five as moderate, one as weak and, importantly, six colleges – including four from the Eastern Cape, constituting half of the colleges in this province – were identified as dysfunctional and in need of a compliance-focused intervention plan (JET, 2012c).

This chapter describes the monitoring and evaluation (M&E) of the CIP using a theory of change approach that established which changes were required to improve the colleges' functionality and enable them to accomplish the tasks expected of them. The chapter also provides insights into what is entailed in measuring the achievements of a complex programme such as the CIP in order to document lessons learnt.

Prior to commencement of the CIP, a number of the dysfunctional colleges were placed under administration at some point during the lifespan of the project in an attempt to create a greater level of compliance. This measure was seen as the DHET's response to the imperative highlighted in the initial assessment, but had unintended outcomes.

In this context, the turnaround of the colleges was considered to require a 'comprehensive' strategy across a wide spectrum of functional domains, including: Strategic and Operational Planning; Management and Governance; Teaching and Learning; Human Resource Management and Development; Finance and Risk Management; the Education Management Information System (EMIS); Student Support Services (SSS); and Physical Infrastructure and Facilities. It was anticipated that the project would tackle four levels of functionality – policies, systems, processes, and capacity – in the aforementioned domains.

Strategic stakeholder relationships and partnerships were also seen as a key element of the successful turnaround of the colleges. Whilst the CIP focused on the different functional areas, the emphasis of the interventions was on the imperative of improving teaching and learning, consistent with the conceptual model developed by JET which sought to place student performance and success at the centre of the intervention and gear all the other interventions towards this (JET, 2013).

---

26 Specialist Manager, JET Education Services at the time of the CIP.

There were smaller and larger changes in the project strategy over time. A key shift occurred when the DHET formed a partnership with the South African Institute for Chartered Accountants (SAICA) to support the colleges with respect to financial and human resources management (JET, 2013). The introduction of SAICA as a partner allowed JET to focus more on the other functional areas outlined above, although JET continued to engage with the aspects of financial and human resources management which are critical to achieving successful teaching and learning. The emphasis on teaching and learning as the focus of all interventions was further sharpened through the output-to-purpose review (OPR) that was conducted by external evaluators contracted by JET and the DHET.

It was also agreed that, to ensure the project's success, JET would work collaboratively with the provincial education departments (PEDs) as well as with the DHET. This collaborative approach was seen as critical to institutionalising and sustaining the interventions beyond the life of the project. The extent that this was found to be possible and the implications for the programme emerge as an area of learning from this intervention.

The following principles were established to guide the implementation of the CIP:

The programme should be a comprehensive college transformation programme; interventions should be coherent and integrated; a developmental approach, starting with the status quo of each individual college and then defining a pathway of development unique and appropriate to each college, should be adopted; building delivery capacity of college staff must be undertaken; the programme must support the colleges' core business of student learning; the programme must be sustainable in order to make a lasting contribution to colleges' performance; a sense of ownership must be built amongst college staff so that they take full responsibility for the colleges' success and welfare; compliance and responsiveness should be facilitated so that colleges are able to comply with the requirements of the regulatory frameworks that govern their operations; and finally, the project must be based on a common vision of and perspectives on delivery – the wide range of activities to be undertaken in the operation of a college must be embodied in a single vision and in a commonly held perspective on the future of the institution.

This chapter is structured in the following way:

Firstly, an introduction to how monitoring and evaluation activities were conceived is presented and reflected in the following sub-sections:

- Monitoring and evaluation;
- Measuring success; and
- Using the CIP's theory of change to assess the achievements.

Secondly, consideration is given as to how and why the objectives were met and the extent to which they were met under the headings:

- The six strategic objectives: achievements and limitations on what could be achieved; and
- The status of the strategic objective indicators.

Thirdly, a discussion of the outcomes of the CIP from the perspective of the M&E exercise is put forward in terms of:

- What worked and what did not; and
- Taking the lessons of the CIP forward.

Monitoring and evaluation

It was agreed between JET and the DHET that the strategic objective – and therefore the success of the project – would be measured by a set of core indicators linked to priorities for the TVET sector as outlined in the National Development Plan (NDP), the DHET's Annual Performance Plans and the Minister of Higher Education's performance agreement. An advantage of this approach was that data pertaining to these indicators was likely to be available as colleges and the DHET are required to report on these priorities. Alignment of the indicators also introduced a political imperative (i.e. urgency to achieve progress). The strategic objective indicators were:

- Enrolment growth (target of 15% per annum);
- Improved throughput (target of 5% over the national rate by the end of 2014);
- Improved certification rate (target of 5% over the national rate by the end of 2014); and
- Increased number of learners placed – this could include workplace exposure or structured workplace-based experience (WBE) during a programme, or a placement upon graduation into a learnership, apprenticeship, internship, or other work opportunity (target of 5% over the national rate by the end of 2014).

The status of these indicators was reviewed at the outset of the project and then at key points during implementation and provided a basis for understanding the extent to which change was realised over the project's lifespan.

Measuring success

As indicated, the project's overarching goal was 'to demonstrate an effective systemic model of FET college improvement that can be replicated throughout the college sector'. Given this, substantial effort was placed on monitoring and evaluation so that processes and learnings (i.e. what worked, what did not work and why) could be documented.

The project had several features of a 'complex' programme: it operated at multiple levels (e.g. individual, classroom, campus, college, and provincial); it involved multiple stakeholders with different perspectives; whilst it aimed to achieve long-term changes, there was also a need for short-term results (Barnes *et al*, 2003); cause and effect relationships were recursive – the implementation and attainment of 'high-level' objectives interacted with the implementation and attainment of 'lower-level' objectives through feedback loops and other recursive mechanisms; and the outcomes were not always known in advance – some were emergent, (i.e. the specific outcomes and the knowledge and means to achieve them emerged during implementation of the intervention) (Rogers,

2008). This created some challenges for documenting the theory of change, developing a logic model, and conducting monitoring and evaluation, which traditionally assesses progress and achievements in relation to what was planned and expected at the outset.

It was understood that as the project was implemented changes might be made with respect to activities, outputs, and outcomes. Importantly, however, the project's success indicators could not be amended. This was to ensure that while learning through implementation was taken into account and any implications for the design of the project could be accommodated, the focus and intention of the project remained consistent. That is, the target was clear from the outset and the evaluation would focus on understanding the extent to which this target was met and, critically, the factors that had contributed towards or hindered the target's achievement. The evaluation would consider the extent to which the activities were implemented as planned and, where there were changes made, why these changes were required and the effect of the changes on the achievement of the project's outcomes and, ultimately, its strategic objective. Documenting what was done and why and capturing and sharing learning was a priority of the monitoring and evaluation process.

The project implementation team was responsible for project monitoring, and internal evaluation of the project was led by JET's M&E Division which was separate from and had an independent reporting line to the project implementation team. Some aspects of the evaluation – such as an independent OPR – were conducted by external evaluators contracted by JET and the DHET.

The evaluation methodologies utilised during the CIP included a rapid assessment of the colleges, a baseline study, an OPR, a formative evaluation, and case studies.

At the outset of the project, the project team undertook a rapid assessment of each of the colleges. This rapid assessment was conducted in the functional areas that had been identified for the project and were to inform the activities that would be prioritised for the programme and for each college.

Baseline reports were developed for the colleges in both provinces. These reports drew on the initial rapid assessments and provided an overview of the status of the colleges in terms of the outcomes and objectives contained in the logic model which was developed to summarise the project's theory of change. However, since the logic model was developed after the rapid assessments had been completed, and was, in fact, informed by the rapid assessments, the rapid assessment reports are not comprehensive reports on the status of each of the activities, outputs, and outcomes outlined in the logic model. Nevertheless, the reports contain rich data relating to the core outcomes specified in the logic model and therefore provide a basis for understanding the changes that occurred during implementation of the CIP.

An OPR initiated by JET to establish whether the improvement model was working and the objectives of the project were being met took place in April 2012.

The OPR was followed by a formative evaluation, including a review of data relating to the strategic objective indicators, was completed in March 2014. The formative evaluation report incorporated the results of surveys that were completed by college management, lecturers, and students. The surveys were initially intended to establish a baseline regarding the perceptions of key stakeholders and included questions pertaining to the project's activities, outputs, outcomes, and their associated indicators contained in the logic model. The baseline could then be used to ascertain whether there were any shifts in perceptions during the course of the project implementation. However, there was a need to link the survey instruments with the project logic model, and since the logic model could only be developed after the rapid assessments had taken place, the surveys could not be conducted at the outset of the evaluation. Further delays due to college holidays and various other factors meant that project activities had already taken place before and occurred during completion of the surveys. Consequently, the survey findings do not provide a true baseline. The results of the surveys were therefore integrated into the formative evaluation report, with the intention that they be used as a basis against which to benchmark further change. The views of stakeholders – specifically college principals, JET staff, and DHET and PED officials – on the changes that had taken place in colleges and the factors that they believed contributed to or hindered the changes were included in the formative evaluation report, and this information was used to support the ongoing development of the intervention.

Following the formative evaluation, six colleges were selected for case studies using the following criteria: including an equal number of Eastern Cape and Limpopo colleges; including colleges which were at different levels of performance (as measured via certification and throughput rates) and having received differing levels of support from the project; and including colleges which could showcase good practices and success in different areas in which the project worked. The purpose of the case studies was to document what was working well, identify good practices for the purpose of sharing, and investigate further the findings of the formative evaluation. The case studies also probed the perceptions of a range of project beneficiaries at various levels (including senior management, management, lecturers, and students) regarding the interventions and support they received from JET. Importantly, the case studies sought to understand what would be required to ensure that improvements and gains experienced by the colleges could be maintained, sustained, and replicated. The data for the case studies were collected through site visits, face-to-face interviews, and focus group discussions at colleges and campuses in May 2014.

The final step in the internal M&E process was the summative evaluation undertaken at the conclusion of the programme and which focused on understanding the progress that the project had made measured against its strategic objectives and indicators. This summative evaluation included an analysis of college enrolment and certification rates, the placement rates of learners, and throughput rates of programmes so that a comparison could be made between the status of the strategic objective indicators at the outset of the project and at the end.

The summative evaluation also reviewed the extent to which the final outcomes envisaged for the programme had been attained and the final report reflects on the extent to which the achievement (or failure to achieve) particular outcomes contributed towards the realisation of the CIP's objectives. Factors that enabled or hindered the process are considered and lessons for similar interventions in the future are indicated. Among the questions which the summative evaluation sought to answer were:

- What is the status of the strategic objective indicators at project close-out and what changes have occurred from 2011 to 2014?

- What has the project produced, delivered, and achieved?
- What changes (positive and negative) have occurred at the colleges in the functional areas on which the project focused, did the project contribute to these changes and, if so, how?
- What challenges and impediments to the project were identified and how did these affect project implementation and success?
- Is it likely that the changes which have occurred will be sustained post the project? What is required for sustainability?
- What is it possible and plausible for a college improvement project such as this to address and what needs to be in place for such a project to succeed?

In order to provide a balanced assessment of the programme's implementation and success, a range of data sources was used, including:

- The theory of change and logic model which was developed for the project and subsequently updated with the project team;
- A review of relevant literature;
- A review of project documents (business plan, quarterly reports, evaluation reports, etc.), and monitoring data;
- A review of secondary data pertaining to the strategic objective indicators provided by the DHET, colleges and, in some instances, JET;
- In-depth case studies of three Eastern Cape and three Limpopo colleges;
- Interviews with members of the JET management and implementing teams;
- Interviews with DHET and PED officials;
- Telephonic interviews with principals or nominated representatives from each of the colleges; and
- Perception surveys conducted with managers, lecturers and students at the colleges in 2013 and again in 2014.

After the closure of the project, an external evaluation of the CIP was commissioned by the DHET and completed in September 2015.

Assessing achievements with the CIP's theory of change

Developing the theory of change for the CIP and reviewing progress was undertaken using a participatory approach. At project inception, a process was followed to document the theory of change. The activities, outputs (deliverables) and outcomes (expected changes) for which the project would be accountable were discussed, and indicators which would demonstrate programme success were developed during a workshop held with the JET project team. These were then shared with and agreed to by the DHET. At key points during the project, the theory of change was reviewed and updated, and what was done and the reasons for amendments were documented.

At the outset of the summative evaluation, the evaluation team conducted theory of change workshops with the JET project team during which the teams considered the theory of change that had been adopted at the outset, reflected on the extent to which the outcomes that had been agreed upon were achieved, and looked at the influencing factors. The evaluation team also assessed whether the projected outcomes were appropriate; in some cases it was felt that the CIP (and JET) should have not been accountable for particular outcomes, since accomplishing them depended on decisions and actions that only the DHET could take, for example, outcomes relating to contracting and procurement.

The relationship between the theory of change, the planning process, and monitoring and evaluation is highlighted in the diagram below:

FIGURE 7 Relationship between theory of change, planning, monitoring and evaluation

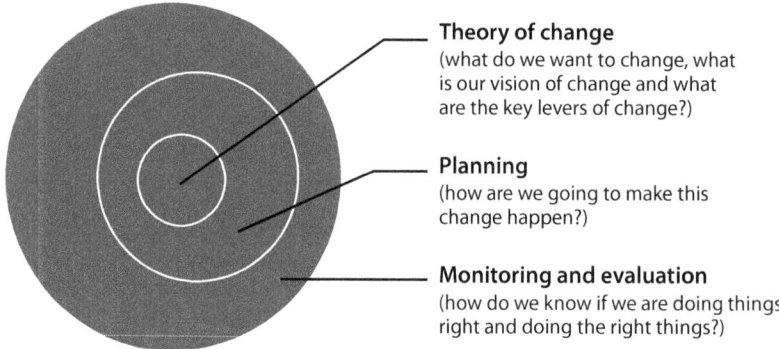

The starting point of developing the theory of change was to understand the key challenges: that is, what needed to be changed. This was achieved by means of a rapid assessment of each of the participating colleges in the two provinces. The rapid assessment findings informed the consideration of what could be changed in this environment and the development of a vision of change (the anticipated impact of the change) for the programme. Further, the way in which this change could be measured was specified. The following four high-level indicators of change (referred to as strategic objective indicators) which coincided with the core indicators linked to the national priorities for the TVET sector, as previously mentioned, were agreed upon. These were the areas the project sought to influence and improve:

- Enrolment;
- Certification rate;
- Throughput rate; and
- Number of learners placed in work/industry.

The JET team then considered how the CIP could contribute to realising changes in these indicators and explored the key levers of change. Based on this analysis, JET determined the key activities to be undertaken and the anticipated outcomes of these activities. The assumptions and risks underpinning the project were also outlined in the theory of change.

As outlined previously, because of the nature of this project, it was recognised that during implementation, the monitoring and evaluation processes would provide insights and learning regarding whether the agreed upon activities were being implemented as planned, whether the activities were resulting in the intended outcomes, and the extent to which the assumptions and risks were proving to be appropriate. These insights resulted in the theory of change being reviewed, and changes in the activities that would be prioritised and the outcomes for which the programme could be held accountable.

The essence of the initial theory of change agreed upon is reflected in the CIP's six strategic objectives and their outcomes which evolved based on learning acquired during the implementation of the project.

Six strategic objectives: Achievements and limitations

Over the three years of implementation, the CIP worked towards six objectives, each of which was broken down into at least six outcomes, with the total number of outcomes approaching 50 in number. The intention here is to summarise progress per strategic objective and to draw attention to constraints on what the CIP could influence.

Objective 1: To improve the quality of teaching and learning in the colleges

It was found during the course of implementation that the extent of the challenge faced in achieving this objective had not been understood, and the intervention could not reach all lecturers. Instead it focused on the subject areas in which the biggest challenges had been identified, and it was agreed that whilst there would be certain interventions that were generic and intended for all lecturers – such as induction and assessment – other interventions would focus primarily on developing the skills of Mathematics lecturers. It was also found that whilst academic heads, in the effort to improve the quality of teaching and learning, could be supported to observe and monitor classes, many did not have time to conduct observations as they were themselves lecturing. This situation raised a question about the assumptions of the programme and led to the conclusion that the job requirements of academic heads needed to be amended and their lecturing time reduced. It was also found that whilst JET could assist lecturers to identify the resources needed to improve the quality of teaching and learning, a number of obstacles involving procurement arose which the programme could not resolve.

Objective 2: To ensure that there are integrated student support services available in the colleges

Establishing integrated student support services which meet the needs of students requires the colleges to have efficient recruitment, selection, and registration processes and information gleaned from entry assessments as to what type of support students require. Other aspects of student support included in this objective were access to financial aid and work-based learning experience. JET initially supported the development of recruitment strategies, guidelines and systems, the streamlining of admission processes and the capturing of registration data. However, as the programme proceeded it was found that the extent of this initiative was too wide and the focus had to be narrowed. Thus JET could only play a nominal role in the support of the pre-counselling process. In addition it was found that, whilst JET could provide support for the registration of students who required financial aid, JET could not influence whether the students actually received financial aid. It was found that in order to achieve the objective of integrated student support services, JET had to focus on piloting innovative ways in which academic support could be provided. JET was able to provide support to the colleges to enable them to monitor assessment results and guide students into support programmes. However, because of the pressure (or in some cases perceived pressure) on colleges to create a space for all students and to expand enrolment numbers, the understanding of many colleges was that they could not deny a student entrance into a particular programme, even if the student did not meet the admission requirements. For this reason, JET could not consistently influence whether the results of the assessments were used to guide students. In addition, JET prioritised supporting a work experience programme for students and also provided some support for a work experience programme for lecturers.

Objective 3: To improve management systems and capacity in the colleges

As indicated, SAICA was allocated responsibility for supporting financial management, changing JET's role with respect to providing support to the financial management functional area. In the course of implementation, JET encountered considerable instability at the level of management. Many of the colleges were placed under administration and in a number of cases the administrator changed during the lifespan of the programme. This meant that the risks associated with management, although recognised at the outset, were considerably higher than anticipated.

Objective 4: To improve governance in the colleges

The objective in this functional area changed substantially during the course of implementation as councils were only put in place in the final year of the strategy. Thus the outcomes associated with governance could not be achieved as it was only possible to begin interventions to train and work with councils in the final phase of the programme. Thus while JET was able, with the support of the DHET, to develop a manual to support council training that focused on enabling councils to understand their roles and functions, it was not possible within the time available to achieve all of the outcomes listed above. While this risk had been considered, the extent of the delay had not been taken into account and this had a negative effect on the effectiveness of the intervention in the functional area of governance.

Objective 5: To ensure effective EMIS are in place

This is an area in which little was amended with respect to the theory of change; supporting EMIS remained a priority for the JET intervention. However, in the course of implementation it was recognised that many of the challenges related to the IT systems that the colleges had in place. Decisions about IT systems were outside of JET's scope and, whilst JET could provide advice with respect to systems, this was an area that ultimately had to be addressed by the colleges and the DHET since it involved issues of procurement and contracts that were in place. It was also found that there were significant challenges with respect to connectivity and this limited the extent to which systems could be integrated across the colleges. Again, while JET was able to provide advice in this regard and support submissions to the DHET, it could not resolve these issues. These risks posed significant challenges with respect to what could be achieved and again pointed to the reality of what a support programme could and could not do.

Objective 6: To improve financial and risk management in the colleges

As indicated previously, this function became the responsibility of SAICA and for this reason was no longer part of the JET programme. JET raised a concern that the relationship with SAICA was not clear and that this undermined JET's ability to ensure that financial planning and management effectively took the needs of teaching and learning into account. However, the relationship had not been effectively forged at a national level. Thus, while there was an indication from JET that engagement with SAICA was possible at some of the colleges, it was not consistently achieved. This tension was also highlighted by some lecturers who raised concerns about the extent to which procurement systems supported the teaching and learning processes. It is therefore suggested that this disjunction, whilst allowing JET to focus on other aspects of the theory of change, may have adversely impacted on the overall intentions of the programme.

Status of strategic objective indicators

Having outlined what the theories of impact and implementation were at the outset of the project and how the implementation theory changed in response to a better understanding of the context, a reduction in the project's scope and a greater focus on areas in which it was felt the project could achieve the best results (bearing in mind time and resource constraints), the chapter turns to a discussion of the strategic objective indicators identified for the programme and their status at the programme's conclusion.

A general finding of the summative evaluation was a massive growth in enrolment numbers, 58.3% across the 15 colleges in just one year. The strain on the system due to this increase is seen in the comparison between certification results in 2011 and 2012. Better run colleges immediately saw the consequence of increasing access in the absence of improvements in infrastructure, lecturer capacity, etc., and decided to play it safe in the following year by not increasing the enrolments so drastically. The result of this decision can be seen in the reasonable increase of 14 270 enrolments recorded between 2012 and 2013 across the 15 colleges, equating to an increase of 13.9%, although between 2013 and 2014 enrolments increased more, by 26 948, equating to an increase of 23.0%.

In relation to the CIP, while enrolment at each college increased over the period 2010 to 2014, the colleges that experienced significant increases in enrolments in the face of limited institutional change and stagnant budgets saw a decline in their results. This highlights the challenges confronted by colleges when they expand dramatically and the negative impact rapid expansion has on teaching quality and ultimately on results.

Certification rates of TVET colleges, the subject of the CIP's second strategic objective, have been historically poor. In 2010 and 2011, the actual national certification rates were below 25% for all programmes and levels, further evidence that expanding enrolment in the absence of quality improvement can have an adverse effect on certification rates. The stagnation and decrease in certification rates also clearly demonstrate the results of the mandate from the DHET to increase student access to colleges in the face of the annual budget remaining unchanged.

The evaluation found that certification rates of the colleges varied over the years during which the CIP was implemented, with certification rates of some colleges improving steadily, some fluctuating, and still others decreasing. Colleges that performed well had well-coordinated year plans in place, ensured conflicts were mediated timeously, and examined learner performance for the previous year, which enabled the colleges to identify subjects in which the learners performed poorly and to plan and implement activities to mitigate the poor performance. As part of this process, these colleges monitored the progress of learner performance on a quarterly basis and provided support to students at risk. While it is reasonable to expect that the JET intervention may have influenced certification rates from 2012, various college-level, provincial, and system-wide factors may have impacted positively or negatively on students' academic performance. For example, limited academic achievement may be attributed to: absence of college councils, colleges being placed under administration, poor leadership and management, high turnover of staff, lecturer disaffection, student unrest, expansion in enrolments, and stagnant budgets.

It is reasonable to expect that the JET intervention may have influenced throughput rates in the Eastern Cape and Limpopo colleges from 2012 onwards, although as with the enrolment and certification data, throughput rate is likely to be affected by a range of other factors.

While throughput data was difficult to ascertain and sometimes incomplete, the evaluation found, encouragingly, that in the Eastern Cape the throughput rates increased between 2012 and 2013 in three out of the four colleges. All colleges for which 2010–2012 data was available had throughput rates above the provincial and national averages and three out of four colleges had throughput rates which were more than 5% above the national average (the target).

The Limpopo colleges' throughput rates for 2010–2012 and 2011–2013 were calculated for five colleges, and for two colleges they were calculated for 2011–2013 only. The throughput rates improved between 2012 and 2013 in three colleges and declined in two, in one dramatically. The 2010–2012 cohort in all five colleges for which data was available performed above the provincial and national averages, with two colleges performing at more than 5% above the national average.

The throughput rate of National Certificate Vocational (NCV) programmes is, overall, poor. While the certification rate at each level may be reasonable, progression to the next level is a challenge. Factors that seem to have contributed to this problem are students changing from NCV to Report 191 programmes (e.g. students who complete NCV2 and then move to a Report 191 programme the following year) and students dropping out altogether.

For students doing the Report 191 programmes, lack of opportunity to gain practical workplace experience impedes their graduation, as work experience is a requirement for completing these courses. Not having work experience also hinders students seeking employment, as they may be unprepared and companies are often unwilling to hire people with no work experience. Expanding young people's access to work experience is thus a key national priority and the fourth strategic objective of the CIP. Government Outcome 5 and the DHET's strategic plan (DHET 2012 and 2013) set the following targets for the increased placement of learners in learnerships, apprenticeships, and workplace experience:

- 20 000 graduates receiving work-integrated learning (WIL) by 2014/2015; and
- 70% of NCV learners receiving workplace experience by 2014.

The CIP increased the number of learners placed in work/industry as its fourth strategic objective. In 2013, the CIP supported colleges with placing NCV4 students in the workplace for a minimum of five days during the college holidays. In the Eastern Cape, in comparison with 380 in 2011, the number of NCV students placed almost doubled to reach 724 NCV4 students in 2013 and increased around fourfold to 1 631 NCV4 students in 2014. This is a remarkable improvement and illustrates what can be done by the college staff to find workplaces to accept students. In 2013, of the 3 202 students enrolled in NCV4 in Eastern Cape colleges, 23% (724) students were placed. In 2014, this doubled to 47%, with 1 631 of the 3 465 students enrolled being assigned to workplaces.

The overall NCV4 placement rate for Limpopo was 55% in 2013 and 78% in 2014. The success of work placement for students in Limpopo culminated in a provincial workplace-based experience (WBE) forum, which will support the colleges in planning, implementing and monitoring WBE after this project comes to an end.

National data is not available from the DHET regarding the numbers and proportions of students placed in WBE, so it is not possible to report in relation to the target set for this strategic objective indicator of 5% above the national rate by 2014.

The placement of students in the workplace was an area that showed great improvement; this is evidenced by the dramatic increase in the numbers of students assigned to workplaces from 2011 to 2013 and again in 2014. The project also played a key role in establishing/strengthening provincial structures where WBE and related issues are discussed. In Limpopo, the province established a WBE forum to continue providing support to the colleges in placing students after the project ends. In the Eastern Cape, the DHET coordinates a forum which brings together the PED, colleges, SETAs, and the Office of the Premier to discuss WBE and other college issues.

What worked and what didn't

One of the important issues raised during the evaluation of the CIP pertains to expectations of what the project should have and could have achieved. The data gathered from the range of interviews conducted for the evaluation provide further insight into where the programme succeeded and where it did not.

An interviewee from JET suggested that the DHET held the view that JET would play the role of department in the two provinces. Yet, as JET interviewees suggested, this was an unrealistic expectation and JET was not in a position to address the challenges in the provinces relating to problems with college CEOs, the absence of college councils, administration difficulties and issues concerning the allocation of the NSFAS bursaries. JET interviewees suggested that JET's ability to work successfully in this environment was dependent on the DHET directly resolving certain issues; JET could then have provided effective support to teaching and learning. Departmental interviewees agreed that the allocation of roles and responsibilities were not clear and commented that the DHET should have had individuals that were responsible for the programme within the department. An interviewee from the DHET observed that the absence of a consistent management structure within the department meant that challenges could not be jointly resolved and that the department struggled to get a clear sense of what the project was achieving. The interviewee observed that the absence of clear reports from JET that succinctly captured what had been done made this an even greater challenge. The evaluation team also confronted the difficulty of obtaining succinct data reflecting the numbers of college staff and students reached by the different training initiatives and, whilst there was a strong sense of the results achieved by the programme, the need for regular reports on results in relation to intended outputs should have been addressed.

Another difficulty that emerged was that although the programme tried to be more focused and concentrate resources on teaching and learning, this still proved to be too wide-ranging a challenge to tackle. As a result, the emphasis of the programme shifted, although not exclusively, to Mathematics teaching and learning (although there was also induction training as well as training in methodologies and assessment). Interviewees all agreed that the focus on teaching and learning and, in particular, on improved lecturer capacity in Mathematics was relevant. They suggested that locating the development interventions for Mathematics within the campus improvement programme was very important as this enabled the colleges to work out what other lecturer support needed to be implemented. Interviewees emphasised, however, that even with the interventions implemented by the colleges and JET, the process of ensuring that lecturers had the relevant competence was a long journey and these interventions only represented a few steps in this journey. Some of the colleges indicated that there was now a greater commitment to continuous development of lecturers, but challenges relating to finance for training and ensuring that lecturers were willing to participate still existed. Further, as indicated previously, there were a number of factors outside of JET's ambit of control, such as the high turnover of lecturers and the low number of lecturers versus the increasing number of students that affected the project's success.

There are some interventions that colleges seemed to be confident about sustaining: a number of colleges felt they could sustain interventions such as the improved enrolment and registration process as this has been institutionalised. Some principals believe WIL will be sustainable as they have established relationships with industry and processes for managing WIL. It was also suggested that the recognition of the importance of campus improvement programmes and the more coordinated approach to management that has been adopted will be sustained.

However, interviewees from across the colleges, JET, and the DHET pointed to a number of important areas which could affect the sustainability of the JET interventions, including loss of institutional memory and the extent to which there had been a sharing of experiences. Interviewees indicated that the challenge of sustainability was exacerbated by the significant amount of institutional instability in the colleges. Some of the college leaders that JET had worked with had left the colleges, 'and it is questionable to what extent the JET experience has been passed onto new incumbents'. A key issue affecting sustainability of the project in the Eastern Cape is that during the JET intervention the majority of Eastern Cape colleges were placed under administration, leading to a high turnover of senior managers. For example, in some colleges an administrator fulfilled the role of 'acting' principal and a number of the acting principals and/or administrators were not fully familiar with the JET intervention. Some acting principals left the colleges in 2014, making it questionable whether the newly appointed principals or acting principals were fully briefed about the JET intervention. This raised the question of whether champions remained in the organisations to spearhead and keep the project learnings alive. This concern is intensified by a number of principals who stated in interviews that they did not feel confident to talk about the JET intervention as they were too new. One interviewee commented on the problem of sustainability and leadership instability, stating, 'one person comes in and we do it this way and then another comes in and we do it another way'.

Some interviewees indicated that they had put managers in charge of interventions that had been introduced by the project and therefore felt that the interventions would persist. However, other interviewees expressed concern that in the absence of champions to drive the processes, some of the interventions would likely not survive; a few interviewees suggested that in the final year of the programme, JET should have focused on putting arrangements in place to ensure the interventions continued. Interviewees were particularly concerned that with the JET programme coming to an end, the support that had been provided to them would be discontinued and the colleges would struggle to pay for the interventions, making it more difficult to sustain them. Some of the principals urged, as a solution, that the 'provincial offices be tasked with the responsibility of taking up where JET has left off'.

A number of principals commented that critical to sustaining the interventions was the continuation of the forums established for colleges to share experiences. One principal pointed out that colleges historically have tended to work in silos and the JET support facilitated a sharing of information and best practices, which helped the college management keep up to date. It was indicated that where forums existed to facilitate sharing and learning, such as in relation to WBE in Limpopo and EMIS in the Eastern Cape, interventions would stand a greater chance of being sustained. Another interviewee commented that the value of the forums was that they created awareness that 'we are not alone and can learn from others on how to deal with the problems we face'. One JET interviewee observed that JET also anticipated that the existence of manuals, guidelines and tools which were developed by the programme, for example on lesson planning and lesson observation, should assist in ensuring the programme's sustainability. However, in certain areas where opportunities to share were not created, sustainability was at risk.

Taking the CIP lessons forward

It is the view of the evaluation team that in order for the colleges to continue to benefit from the changes brought about by the CIP, the DHET needs to institutionalise those innovations that it wishes to sustain: for example, if the campus improvement plans are to be sustained, the DHET must inform colleges that they are expected to develop and implement these plans and that reports on the interventions that emanate from the plans will be required. Similarly, the DHET must give colleges a deadline for putting in place their peer tutoring programmes.

If the CIP support project is to be replicated as originally intended, there is a need to consider what can be achieved and by when: in an intervention as wide-ranging as this one, there should be a joint structure to manage the project, solve problems collectively, and determine what actions need to be taken and who is responsible. Importantly, there is a need to agree on the minimum conditions that must be in place to enable such an intervention to work. The CIP experience illustrates that it was not possible to intervene in the way that was planned without stable management and leadership in place, willing to support and enable change in the colleges. The successful interventions undertaken during the CIP should be noted and considered: the registration process; campus improvement plans and the link with lecturer development (including shadowing other lecturers who have shown success); peer tutoring; and support for WBE. It is recommended that these initiatives be rolled out across all colleges in a way that ensures that the learning that was acquired by the colleges that participated in the CIP is shared with colleges across the country.

References

Barnes, M., Matka, E., & Sullivan, H. (2003). Evidence, Understanding and Complexity Evaluation in Non-linear Systems. *Evaluation*, 9(3): 265–284.

Department of Higher Education and Training. (2012). *Annual Performance Plan 2012/2013*. Pretoria: DHET.

Department of Higher Education and Training. (2013). *Delivery Agreement 5: A skilled and capable workforce to support an inclusive growth path*. Pretoria: DHET.

International Labour Organization. (2006). *Global employment trends for youth*. Geneva: ILO.

JET Education Services. (2012a). FET: Eastern Cape baseline, unpublished evaluation report.

JET Education Services. (2012b). FET: Limpopo baseline, unpublished evaluation report.

JET Education Services. (2012c). *FET College Improvement Programme: Frameworks, approaches and capacity*. Status report on the FET Colleges Improvement Project to the DHET, November 2012.

JET Education Services. (2013). Output-to-Purpose Review of the FET College Improvement Project, Final report, 17 April 2013.

JET Education Services. (2014). Formative evaluation report of the FET Colleges Improvement Project, unpublished evaluation report.

JET Education Services. (2015). TVET colleges Improvement Project: September 2011 – December 2014: project close-out report, draft document.

JET Education Services/Department of Higher Education and Training. (2013). DHET FET Colleges Improvement Project Business Plan: November 2013 – December 2014 draft document.

National Planning Commission. (2011). *National development plan 2030: Our future, make it work.* Pretoria: NPC.

Pote, N. (2014). Chief Director: National Examinations and Assessment, DHET, 2014, personal communication, 25 February 2014.

Republic of South Africa. (2006). *Further Education and Training Colleges Act, 16 of 2006.* Pretoria: Government Printers.

Rogers, P. (2008). Using Programme Theory to Evaluate Complicated and Complex Aspects of Interventions. *Evaluation,* 14(1): 29–48.

Statistics South Africa (StatsSA). (2014). *National and provincial labour market: Youth.* Statistical release P0211.4.2. Pretoria: Statistics South Africa.

www.ingramcontent.com/pod-product-compliance
Lightning Source LLC
Chambersburg PA
CBHW060420300426
44111CB00018B/2917